Stick Child's Greatest Hits

Stick Child's Greatest Hits

How Not to Suck at Performance Management

Simon Guilfoyle

Copyright © 2023 Simon Guilfoyle

All rights reserved

ISBN: 979-8-395-04876-9

London, England

Table of Contents

Introduction

Understanding Targets (For the Under-10s)   1

Right Measures, Measured Right   5

This Time Last Year   9

Stick Child's Guide to Systems Thinking   13

Spot the Difference   16

Leadership is Not Enough   23

Stick Child's School Project   25

94/6   29

It's Criminal   33

Top of the Table   37

Straight Lines   42

Maths Class	46
Stick Child's Guessing Game	53
Three Different Things	58
Stick Child Tries to Buy Milk	61
On Purpose	65
The People vs The System	69
What's Your Poison?	71
Lose Weight with Systems Thinking	74
The Weather Man	79
Avoidable Harm	82
A Tale of Two Kings	87
Comfort Blanket	91
How to Quit	93
The Wrong Conversation	97

Stick Child and the Flat Tyre	102
Detox	105
Finding the Source	108
Short Circuit	115
Stick Child's Kitchen Nightmares	117
Why Year-to-Date is Rubbish	122
The Professionals	130
A Better Way	133
About the Author	139

Introduction

Between 2011 and 2016 I authored a light-hearted blog about performance management (mainly in policing). You can view it here:

> **www.inspguilfoyle.wordpress.com**

I talked about the benefits of Systems Thinking, as well as the damage caused by numerical targets, league tables and other forms of simplistic performance measurement.

Eventually, I hit upon the idea of creating *Stick Child* and his little band of *Stick People* to break down some of these simple performance management concepts to a level that *'even a 10-year-old could understand'*.

Sadly, some senior leaders still seem unable to grasp these extremely straightforward ways of understanding organisational systems and improving performance, so I thought it might be timely to compile a few of my old blog posts in a little book.

You might find the content useful, or it might just make you smile and help you to stay sane.

Simon Guilfoyle

Understanding Targets (For the Under-10s)

This is Stick Child.

Stick Child is just nine years old. Awww.

Stick Child wants to understand about targets, so he plays a game...

Stick Child likes paper planes, so he sets himself a target of making one in 60 seconds. How did he get this number? Well, he invented it in his head because it sounds nice. This is also how grown-ups decide targets.

Now, poor little Stick Child tried his hardest, but he just couldn't make a paper plane in less than 85 seconds. This made him feel very sad.

When his Grandma asked him if he had been able to make one in less than 60 seconds, he did a naughty thing and told her that he had managed to do it, even though this wasn't true. Afterwards, Stick Child realised this wasn't the right thing to do and felt bad.

Later on, Stick Child's Daddy asked him why he looked so sad. Stick Child said he felt sad because he hadn't told the truth to Grandma and he was very sorry. Daddy sat Stick Child on his knee and explained that numerical targets often cause this type of dysfunctional behaviour, but that it didn't necessarily mean he was a bad kid. Then he gave him a cuddle.

Better still, Stick Child's Daddy showed him how to fold paper quickly to make really good paper planes that fly well. He also showed him lots of designs in a book, which meant that Stick Child could learn how to make lots and lots of really good paper planes.

Stick Child practiced making paper planes and he became very good at it. He found that he was able to make some planes in as little as 25 seconds; others took longer, because they were a bit more complicated, but that didn't matter because they were really good planes.

This made Stick Child very happy. He was able to show his Grandma his planes and this made her happy too. Stick Child's Daddy told him that although his 60 second target sounded nice, it didn't actually help him make paper planes any better or quicker because *targets do not provide a method.*

Now Stick Child knows the way to become good at something is to learn about that thing, find a way to do the thing really well, and always do your best. He also learnt that targets make people do naughty things, even when they aren't bad people.

If Stick Child can understand this, so can you.

Right Measures, Measured Right

...is a phrase I often use when talking about measuring stuff in performance systems. Although I deride arbitrary numerical targets, I genuinely believe it's essential to measure things, as long as they are the right things.

So, first of all, that begs the question, *"What are the 'right things'?"*

Well, to begin with, the right measures are the ones derived from *purpose.* Purpose is what the system is there to achieve.

For instance, here are some dials in a cockpit. I've marked what a few of them tell the pilot.

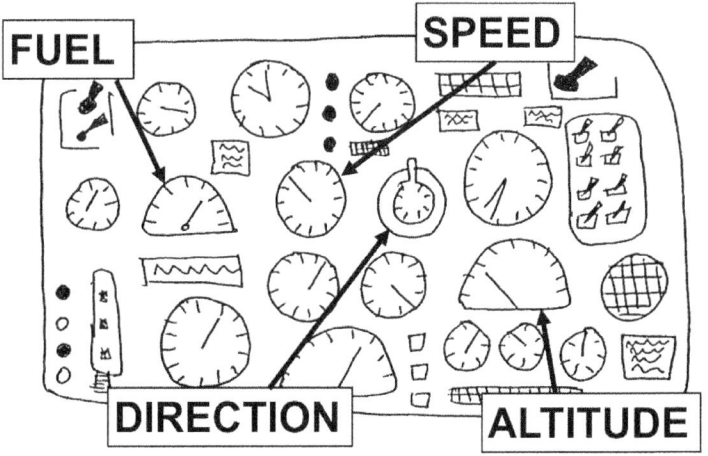

You can see that it's pretty useful stuff – how fast the plane is flying, what direction it's heading, how much fuels it's using, and so on. All linked to *purpose* – in this case to fly passengers safely to their destination. The method by which the information is relayed to the pilot is useful too – the dials are capable of indicating change in real time, enabling our pilot to respond accordingly and make adjustments if necessary.

Right measures, measured right.

Therefore, the right measures, presented in a meaningful and readable format, enable the user to understand how the system is performing, as well as identify what needs to be done to attain purpose successfully.

Now, what about if you use the wrong measures?

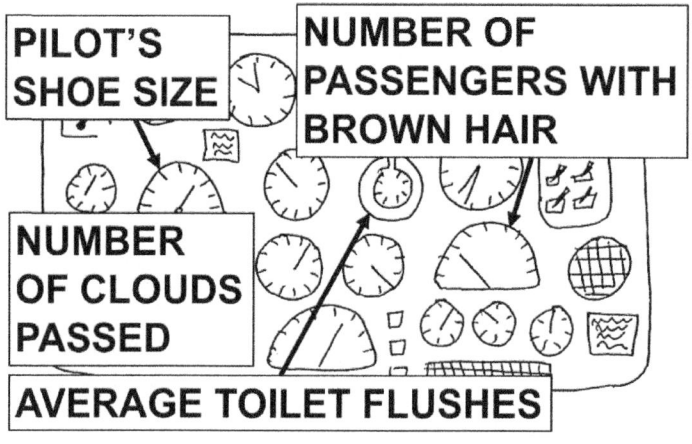

Well here's the same set of dials, this time configured to measure the wrong things. Ok so it's a pretty daft example, but it makes the point. Using the wrong measures means it's impossible to establish if you're achieving purpose. There's no point counting the wrong things, just because they're easy to count. Furthermore, if you're using the wrong measures, don't expect them to encourage the right behaviours.

Next, what about if you measure the right things, but in the wrong way? Well, this happens:

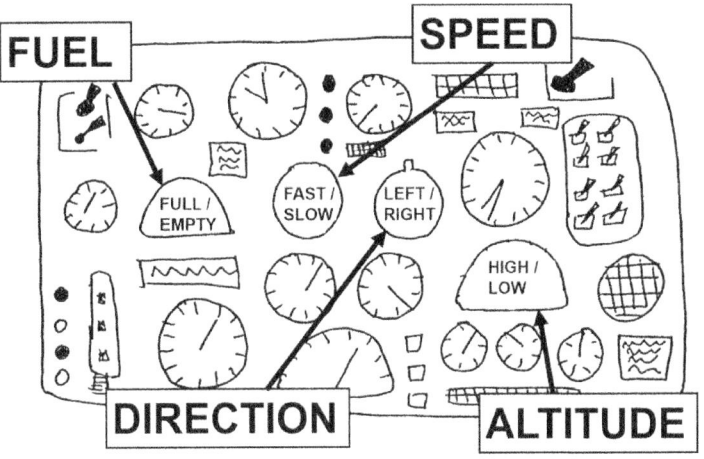

Here's the 'binary comparison' version of the cockpit dials. All the same measures as in the original configuration, but presented in a way that can't tell you anything useful.

Finally, for the benefit of those people who interpret my 'no targets' message as 'no performance management', relax - I'm not some kind of anti-measurement anarchist;

This is what would happen if we didn't measure anything:

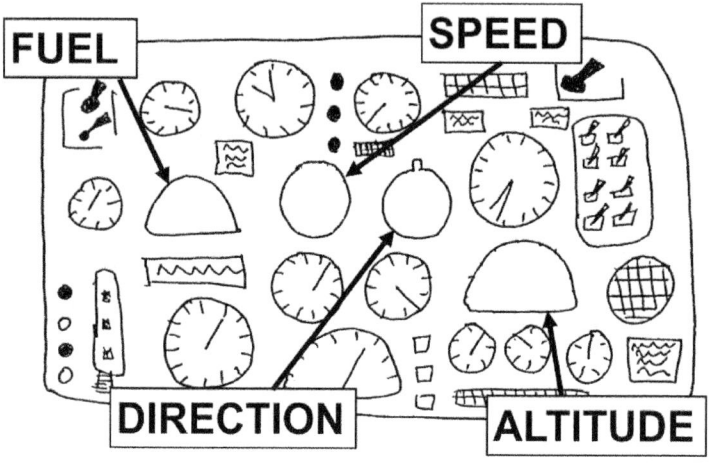

I wouldn't want to be a passenger on that plane.

There's nothing pink and fluffy about doing measurement properly. It's just better use of information. Much better than trying to guess whether something's going up or down because you've compared it to last month. And taking the targets out means that people can focus on purpose, rather than the targets.

Enjoy the flight!

This Time Last Year

Question: What have these four things got in common?

1. Choosing a random number generated by a lottery machine.

2. Reading tea leaves.

3. Blindfolding yourself and sticking a pin in a board.

4. Tossing a coin.

Answer: They're all better methods of informing your decision-making than using this:

CRIME TYPE	2021	2022	CHANGE	% CHANGE
BURGLARY	908	851	-57	↓ -6.3%
ROBBERY	340	382	+42	↑ +12.4%
ASSAULT	1,146	1,381	+235	↑ +20.5%
CRIMINAL DAMAGE	1,503	1,420	-83	↓ -5.6%
ALL CRIME TYPES	19,311	21,541	+2,230	↑ +11.5%

e is the sort of thing that sometimes appears in rformance documents. People get paid a lot of money to read these tables and make decisions about resourcing, funding and operational deployments, based on their assessment of the performance data such tables contain. Imagine it's you. What would you prioritise?

Well, perhaps criminal damage isn't such an issue at the moment as it's 'going down', so you could ignore that for the time being and maybe put more emphasis on tackling assaults, which seem to be raging out of control. So, you throw some extra resources at the assault problem and leave the criminal damage and burglaries to look after themselves for a while.

Easy isn't it? Now you've got your priorities sorted what else could you do? Well, one obvious choice is to look at the crime types that are going up and find someone to hold to account. What on earth is the local police commander playing at, by allowing total crime to rise by 11.5%? Maybe he or she should be replaced with someone who actually knows what they are doing!

So, you shuffle some of your people around, take a bit of funding from here, divert a bit from there, have some 'strong words' about performance expectations, and hey presto, everything's hunky dory. Or so it seems, until next time you are shown a similar performance chart and lots of the stuff that was going down is now going up. Time for more strong words, this time aimed at you.

Ooops! Should have read the tea leaves. It's a much more stable and scientific method of assessing performance than using one of these daft tables featuring nice 'up' and 'down' arrows (and sometimes red and green boxes too).

This method of comparing data is known as making a 'binary comparison', and when used as a technique for judging performance, it always gives completely false and meaningless readings. Its main weakness is that it doesn't actually tell you anything about performance.

Performance data should enable you to assess actual performance so that you can make informed decisions that hopefully lead to improvements. The clue is in the name. Comparing just two numbers with each other can never achieve this.

This is what a binary comparison looks like on a chart:

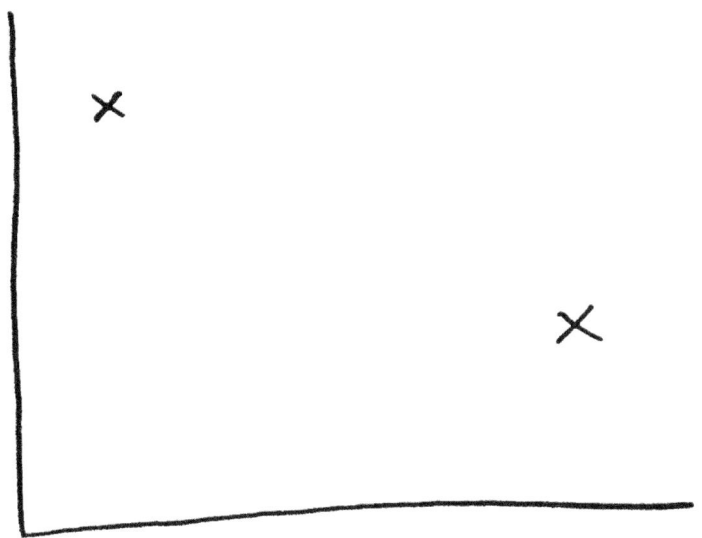

Hopeless, isn't it? It could be 'this year vs last year', 'this month vs last month', 'this week vs last week', or any other similarly useless comparison between two snapshots in time.

This method is rubbish because it discards all the other data points that should be visible between the two points chosen, as well as due to the fact that all data points are subject to non-significant, statistical fluctuations (i.e. normal variation); this means you might as well compare today's figure against any other figure that has ever gone before it. Or a moving object. Or a banana.

The binary comparison approach is commonplace and seen in everyday life - for example:

"Dog bites are up by 4.6% compared to last year".

"Unemployment fell by 15,000 compared to last month".

"Sales figures are up 3.5% compared to last quarter".

"Crime is down 2.3% compared to the same period last year".

In all cases it's meaningless, as the method relies upon scant data, moving variables and unstable assumptions, all of which lead to defective decision-making. Waste is driven into the system because managers react to something that essentially isn't there; costs go up, managers knee-jerk, people are unfairly held to account and performance gets worse.

So... ditch your tables of numbers, 'up' and 'down' arrows, red and green boxes, and use methods that actually tell you something about performance instead.

Stick Child's Guide to Systems Thinking

"What is systems thinking?"

Well, Stick Child's latest piece of homework was to find out about systems thinking, and fortunately his Daddy knows a bit about the subject, so the pair of them sat down together and came up with a simple guide. Here are some of the main points they came up with:

Firstly, Stick Child learnt that there are lots of different strains of 'systems thinking'. Some of them are very complex and theoretical, but Stick Child and his Daddy particularly like the work of renowned management thinker, *W. Edwards Deming*, as it's pretty simple and easy to apply in real life. Deming described a system as:

> *"A network of interdependent components that work together to try and accomplish an aim".*

The important thing is that these interdependent components must *cooperate*, otherwise everyone looks after their own interests and the system breaks down. This means that the customer or service user loses out, which is bad.

Therefore, it's really important that we are absolutely clear about the aim of the system; for example, a hospital might seek to 'help people get better', whilst the police try to 'prevent crime and catch offenders'. In fact, some systems can have lots of aims – in the case of the police, they do lots of things that have nothing to do with crime; these things are also very important.

Stick Child learnt that there is no single 'right' interpretation of systems thinking and that there is a lot of common ground between the various systems thinking approaches.

He also found out that measurement is really important in systems thinking. He learnt that we need to measure things that are happening within the system to understand how it is performing, but that they must be the *right measures*, measured in the *right way*. Stick Child knows that one of the best ways to measure things can be by using *control charts*.

Stick Child also discovered that some people can't tell the difference between 'targets' and 'measures' and this prevents them from being able to understand some really important stuff about how systems work. He wonders if there's a special medicine they could take that would help their brains.

Stick Child learnt that well-meaning people sometimes use really bad ways of trying to measure things, like *binary comparisons*. He also found out *numerical targets* and *league tables* make people put effort into outdoing each other instead of concentrating on the real aim of the system. Sometimes they even cheat and tell lies. Stick Child's Daddy says that this is because numerical targets are *arbitrary* and cause *dysfunctional behaviour*.

Next, Stick Child discovered that *waste* is activity that slows the system down and doesn't help to achieve its aim. There are many types of waste – *failure demand* and *rework* are types of waste that occur because something wasn't done properly the first time round. Waste also occurs when demand that shouldn't be there in the first place enters the system, or when people within the system invent work for others to do, like writing lots of plans, or making them go to meetings where nothing useful occurs.

Stick Child thinks it would be better to put this effort into actually *doing* the work, rather than writing about it or talking about it. He does, however, accept that this might be a radical concept for some people.

Stick Child came to realise that the *thinking* part of systems thinking is really important. He learnt that management thinking needs to change in order for systems-oriented approaches to succeed. He understands that if we keep doing the same things we will keep getting the same results.

That's why we need to remove the bad things that hurt the system, then redesign it so that all the different bits work together to achieve its *aim*, whether this be helping people to get better when they are poorly, or catching baddies.

Spot The Difference

Sometimes when I say this...

...people hear this:

Not being able to differentiate between targets, measures and priorities is a deadly obstacle to effective performance. Let me explain why...

Targets

First of all, if you've ever met me, heard me speaking, or read any of my stuff, you'll have come across my theory on targets. It's straightforward. Only two bits to it. Here's a reminder:

1. All numerical targets are arbitrary
2. No numerical target is immune from causing dysfunctional behaviour

The reason that all numerical targets are arbitrary is because there is no known scientific method of setting one. The traditional method of setting a target usually involves simply looking at last year's performance then adding or subtracting a few percent. That's it.

As a 'method', this is rubbish because it disregards the capability of the system and natural variation. It ignores all the fluctuations in the data that have occurred during the previous 12 months. It means that the 'benchmark' chosen is unstable and the assumption about performance is therefore flawed.

It assumes that the system knows the target is there and will respond to it (it doesn't and it won't!) It ignores the fact that the greatest opportunity for improving performance lies in making systemic adjustments rather than berating, comparing, or otherwise trying to 'motivate' the workers to achieve the target. That's the first part of the theory.

Next, when you hear people say that targets have an effect on performance, they're right. Targets make performance *worse*. This brings us to the second part of the theory...

Targets change behaviour. Rather than collectively focusing on achieving the system's *purpose*, individuals and departments are inadvertently placed into competition with each other, meaning that they turn their effort and ingenuity inward and focus attention on what the target makes them concentrate on.

This happens at the expense of other important aspects of work that are not subject of targets. Numerical targets cause inter-departmental rivalries, gaming, data distortions, higher costs, lower morale, worse service delivery and all manner of other horrible consequences.

There are numerous papers and studies which demonstrate that these things predictably occur when targets are introduced into the mix. I know of no numerical target that is immune from causing such dysfunctional behaviour, hence part two of the theory.

Measures

Unlike targets, measures are really important. Unless you measure stuff happening in your system it is impossible to know how it is performing. The key is in this phrase:

Right measures, measured right!

First of all you need to determine measures that are derived from *purpose*. This means understanding what your system is there to do (e.g. 'to help people and catch baddies' / 'to produce great widgets' / 'to help kids learn about stuff'), then ensure that your measures help to tell you whether you are doing this.

If you choose the wrong measures you will never learn anything about how your system is really performing. Worse still, if you choose the wrong measures it makes people do the wrong things.

If you choose the right measures, you're on the way! Next, all you have to do is measure them *right*. Don't rely on 'this year vs last year' / 'this month vs last month' / 'today vs yesterday' to assess performance (or anything else for that matter).

Why? Because it's pants. It doesn't tell you anything about performance. It ignores variation. It only enables performance to be envisioned in one of two ways – 'good' or 'bad' / 'better' or 'worse' etc.:

...and that's as about much use as a chocolate fireguard if you're trying to understand your system. Judging performance by making such *binary comparisons* leads to terrible decision-making and wasteful, unnecessary deployments. Don't do it!

Instead, plot your data using one of these:

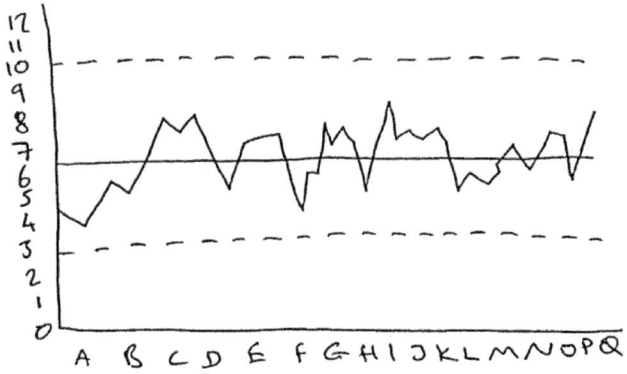

It's a lovely *control chart* (or SPC chart). Without boring you with the science bit, this wonderful invention tells you about the actual performance of your measures. It provides a 'voice' for your system to tell you what's happening. Unless there are recognised signals or trends in the data (e.g. if a data point shoots out of one of the *control limits*), then usually it's best not to react if the zig zags go up or down a bit. This is just *normal variation* and is seen in any set of data, whether you are tracking crime rates, widget production, or the number of red cars that drive past your house every day.

The key is to intelligently interpret the data from the measures – use the information to understand the capability of your system, look for recognised trends (if there are any) and identify opportunities for improving future performance through systemic changes.

When used in this manner, the right measures provide you with an evidence base from which to make decisions, initiate systemic adjustments and determine priorities. Which leads us to...

Priorities

If priorities are established from an evidence base (such as described above) you will be addressing the right things. These are the things that are linked to *purpose* from the customer or service user's perspective. In policing, we like to stop crime from happening, so it could be argued that 'to reduce violent crime' is an appropriate priority for the police.

If 'to reduce violent crime' is therefore designated as a priority, it makes sense to track the rate of violent crime as a measure. If this measure is *measured right*, it enables us to see the true extent of violent crime and respond accordingly.

Three Different Things

Therefore, we have a *priority* which is underpinned by appropriate *measures*. I never trash priorities or measures – they help us keep the system on course to achieve its purpose.

The problem comes where your priority has a numerical target tagged on to it, for example:

> *'To reduce violent crime by 9%'.*

Why? Nowhere do you need a numerical target.

And don't worry, if you take that target away, nothing bad will happen.

It will if you leave it there though.

So, next time you hear me saying we should abandon numerical targets, listen carefully – I'm not saying 'targets AND measures AND priorities'. Just targets.

In summary:

- Priorities are important (when evidence based).

- Measurement (when done properly) is necessary.

- Numerical targets are bad.

Leadership Is Not Enough

Much is made of the importance of leadership, and I don't disagree. However, what's often overlooked is the importance of *system conditions*. Deming talked about this when he pointed out most troubles and opportunities for improvement come from the system. Think about it like this...

Imagine yourself as the world's most inspirational leader. Here you are (in stick person form), trying to achieve your objective of standing these skittles upright.

Unfortunately, they keep tipping over. This is nothing to do with your leadership ability, but simply because the floor surface is slightly convex. No matter how hard you try, they tip over and you spend your time flitting between them, rebalancing them one-by-one as they fall. The uneven floor is a *system problem* – and Deming tells us that managers have the responsibility of addressing system problems. Leadership is not enough.

Here's another example. You're the captain of a ship. Sadly, the ship they put you in charge of has big holes in the hull which keep letting in water. You spend all your time and energy bailing out the water. Your crew work hard for you and you do your best to lead them, but you have no means of repairing the holes. Another system problem. Leadership is not enough.

Last one. Imagine a plant trying to reach its full potential inside a plant pot that it has outgrown. You're expected to tend to it but aren't allowed to re-pot it. Frustrating huh? Well, that's another system condition no amount of your outstanding leadership can fix. Your management have the responsibility of improving the system conditions (i.e. providing you with a bigger plant pot) so that you can demonstrate what a great gardener you are. Leadership is not enough.

Of course, this applies at every level and goes all the way to the top. You can lead within the parameters set for you; those further up the food chain can do the same. But until adverse system conditions are addressed by those at the top of the pile:

Leadership is not enough.

Stick Child's School Project

Over the last few weeks, our little friend Stick Child has been doing a really interesting school project about a thing called *variation*. Not everyone knows about variation. His project is called:

"Understanding Variation (For the Very Young or Pathologically Resistant)".

Stick Child has learnt some pretty cool stuff during his project, which he thinks might be useful for grown-ups who struggle to use numbers properly when it comes to trying to understand performance information.

Here's what he's been up to...

Armed with clip-boards and pencils, Stick Child and his friends have been standing outside their school and counting the number of red cars that drive past on different days. First of all, Stick Child ended up with a nice tally chart, then he used the daily totals to make an even nicer *control chart* like this one:

by Stick Child, aged 9

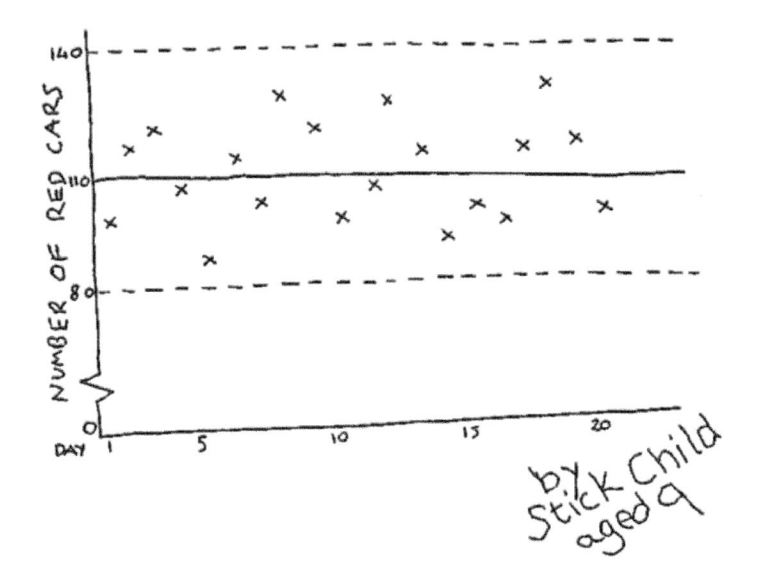

As you can see, there were different amounts of red cars each day. Stick Child's teacher showed the class where the special dashed lines belong on the chart, and explained that in this case, every 'X' between them is completely normal because of this thing called 'variation'. This means it's a mistake to assume there's any meaning behind different individual values, as well as a big waste of time trying to find out why one is different from another.

Next, Stick Child did some experiments with his chart. First of all, he randomly picked one of the numbers between the lines and called it a *target*. Then he tried to work out why sometimes the number of red cars hit the target and sometimes it didn't.

Next, he tried to make the target influence the number of red cars by shouting at the chart and / or the cars as they drove past, but that didn't work either.

Then, he said he would give 10p to one of his friends if she was able to make the target work. At first this didn't make any difference, but later his friend said the target had been met. Stick Child looked closely at her chart and discovered that she had altered some of the numbers on it, so he told the teacher and kept his 10p.

Next, Stick Child picked random previous days' totals on the chart and drew arrows between then to try and work out if the number of red cars was increasing or decreasing. Unfortunately, this just caused confusion because he got a different result every time; he quickly determined that making such *binary comparisons* was rubbish, so stopped doing it.

Finally, Stick Child's teacher timed how quickly the children had drawn their charts, then ranked them in a league table. Then she told the children that half of them were below average. None of the children could understand why she would do this, as they had worked very hard on their projects. It made them feel sad.

After a minute, the teacher told them this was actually just part of the lesson and that really she was very pleased they had done their best, because this is what really matters. Stick Child and his friends were glad that this silly way of assessing performance would never actually happen in real life.

The project taught Stick Child and his friends lots of useful things. He learnt that there is no point worrying about why the total number of red cars was different on different days – this happens because of that thing called variation. He found out that unless *systems conditions* change (e.g. due to a road closure), those little 'X's will continue to appear anywhere between the dashed lines.

In addition to this, Stick Child and his friends learnt that targets don't make any difference to the amount of red cars that drive past his school. This is because variation doesn't pay any attention to man-made follies, such as numerical targets. He remembered his Dad always says that numerical targets are arbitrary and likely to cause dysfunctional behaviour.

Stick Child also discovered that there is no point drawing arrows between two isolated numbers because it gives the impression of trends that simply do not exist. Finally, he learnt that league tables are a poor way of assessing performance. For his efforts, the teacher sent a nice letter to his parents.

Even though he is only nine, Stick Child knows that control charts do not just apply to red cars or school projects. They can also be used by grown-ups, for things like crime figures, response times, or almost any other set of numbers you might want to learn about. (That's if the grown-ups *really* want to learn about these things).

If Stick Children can understand this, so can Big People.

94/6

Deming talked about how about 94% of performance is down to the system and only about 6% attributed to the people within it. This might fly in the face of conventional thinking, but let me give you an example of why it's true:

I'm a fast(ish) police response driver. I drive as quickly and safely as I can to emergencies to help people and catch baddies. Performance targets for response times mean nothing to me because they change nothing about how I drive.

If I or other police response drivers don't get there within the target time it's usually due to *systems conditions* outside of our control, such as the proximity of resources, amount of police units available, road conditions, traffic conditions, the weather and so on.

Systems conditions!

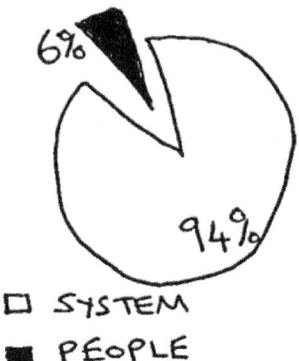

Causes of Performance

- ☐ System — 94%
- ■ People — 6%

Yet most performance management focuses on the individual. "Why did Team 'A' fail to get to three Grade 1 jobs (or immediates / whatever you might know them as) yesterday?" It's that 'WHO's to blame?' mentality again. It MUST be a 'person problem'!

Well perhaps the police station is at the wrong end of the division. Maybe there aren't enough bobbies on response to meet predictable demand. Perhaps an unhelpful deployment policy or lack of vehicles stops them from deploying effectively. Chances are, it's a systems condition.

Consequently, in these circumstances it's wrong to blame individuals. I refer you to the pie chart above. The exact percentages are probably unquantifiable in complex systems such as policing, but they're aren't worth arguing about – the principle itself is solid.

Remember: *The <u>system</u> is always responsible for the majority of performance.*

Then there's the stuff about *methods*. Deming was fond of saying, "By what *method?*"

This is because if you want to see performance improvements you need to have an actual *method* for achieving them. This means understanding the system and improving system conditions to help the workers deliver excellent performance; no amount of inspirational leadership (or sheer hard work) can achieve this if system conditions constrain the workforce.

Therefore, unless we assume frontline workers are bad and lazy, it should be obvious that the way to improve response times is to use data about current performance to inform evidence-based decisions about how to improve the system.

Actual *methods* could include increasing resources in a particular location in response to predictable demand, deploying differently, creating capacity by 'switching off' inappropriate demand, or something else. But you always need a *method*.

Which brings us to response time targets. Putting aside the arguments that numerical targets are arbitrary and prone to causing dysfunctional behaviour, a critical further point is that targets do not provide a *method*. Neither do they provide additional capacity for achieving the improvements sought.

Consequently, just setting an arbitrary numerical target for response times (or anything else), simply does not change anything about those systems conditions that dictate predictable levels of performance. The system will produce what it's capable of producing, whether the target is there or not.

The pro-targets assumption seems to be that if response drivers just worked a bit harder then we'd see improved response times. Well put yourself in their position – you're driving to the incident with blue lights and sirens blaring – does the presence of a target change the distance you have to travel, the road conditions, the weather, your driving ability, the availability of suitable vehicles, the amount of resources on duty, the fact that there are roadworks on one of the main thoroughfares?

Of course not. The target is irrelevant, because it does not provide a *method*.

So, if you want faster response times, safer hospitals, improved service or happier customers, the best way to achieve it is through building an effective *system* and implementing a *method* to achieve good performance- not just telling the workers to work harder, setting targets, blaming individuals, or holding people to account.

It's Criminal

I've often pondered the issue of using crime figures as an indicator of police performance. Aside from the risk of mis-recording crime due to target-driven performance management, I believe there is a fundamental argument against judging police performance by using crime figures. It boils down to this:

> ***"Crime rates are not the definer of effective police performance; they merely provide information about criminal activity".***

What do I mean by this?

Well, we've been so used to judging police performance based on whether crime is higher or lower than some historical point (binary comparisons), positions in league tables, or variance from arbitrary numerical targets, that it's easy to miss the obvious question about whether we're measuring the right thing in the first place.

Even when crime trends are shown in time series format (e.g. control charts), I'd argue that it's still a case of measuring the wrong things (albeit in the 'right' way) if the intention is to assess police performance.

Try these analogies:

- Judging a vehicle repair agency (such as the AA) by the number of breakdowns reported.
- Judging a heart surgeon's performance by the rate of heart disease cases in a locality.
- Judging the fire service's performance by the number of car fires.
- Judging Stick Farmer's performance by the number of lambs born each spring.

(One of these measures is actually real, silly though this may sound).

I'm not saying these datasets are useless for helping people understand their business (they'd certainly be useful for understanding demand and maybe assisting future planning), but they are not measures of *performance*.

In the policing context, yes of course we want to reduce crime (Peel talked about it, didn't he?) and we should take reasonable steps to prevent it, but we need to move beyond the simplistic narrative of:

"Crime up = Police bad / Crime down = Police good".

It's also necessary to acknowledge that multiple factors affect crime rates, such as economic cycles, substance abuse, the weather, societal influences, changes in legislation, and so on. None of these are directly within the gift of the police to influence. Also, what about where the police cause an *increase* in reported crime by having the temerity to find someone carrying a weapon?

Surely proactive policing, or other problem-solving approaches, should not be discouraged on the basis that finding hitherto unreported criminal offences is incongruous with an over-simplified crime reduction narrative.

Look at this like this:

At the local level, if Stick Burglar is arrested and jailed, and burglaries suddenly stop, it's probably fair to assume that the police directly affected that particular crime series. Conversely, at force or national levels, if crime happens to go up or down a bit, it's likely to be as a result of the plethora of external factors that influence the crime rate (as well as normal variation).

It's time for a shift in thinking about crime rates and police performance. By removing perverse incentives for mis-recording crime, we should hopefully be left with a clearer picture of criminal activity. Such data can then act as extremely useful sources of information that assist decision making about how best to tackle reported crime.

But it's not 'performance' data.

In the same way, the AA should not be held accountable for a vehicle breaking down; neither should the fire service be blamed if an electrical fault causes it to catch fire. There may be opportunities to learn about causes and respond to future patterns of demand (where it's predictable), but that's all.

Therefore, it doesn't seem logical to directly equate police effectiveness with crime levels, especially as the true extent of crime is unknown, and what is known is affected by a multitude of factors.

Reported crime, from whatever source, is potentially useful information about criminal activity.

Not performance data.

Top of the Table

When the Chair of the House of Commons Education Committee asked Michael Gove (Secretary of State for Education at the time) about comparative performance measurement between schools, this happened:

> Chair: *If "good" requires pupil performance to exceed the national average, and if all schools must be good, how is this mathematically possible?*
>
> Michael Gove: *By getting better all the time.*

Now, sniggers to one side, there's a few important points here. The first is that I don't disagree with striving to get better all the time; neither do I think performance shouldn't be measured. I also believe it can be useful to understand apparent differences in comparative peer performance. So, what's the problem?

Well, it's the way it's so often done – league tables.

League tables are another simplistic, misleading charlatan of the performance measurement world; they purport to convey information about comparative peer performance, when in fact they produce little more than mirages. They lie to you. They tell you stuff that isn't there. They set you off on thought processes and assumptions that are utterly unwarranted. (A bit like slightly more elaborate binary comparisons. Ugh!) But the most dangerous thing about them is that they appear so plausible.

Here's an example using police forces, although you could replace them with schools, hospitals or other institutions, if you like.

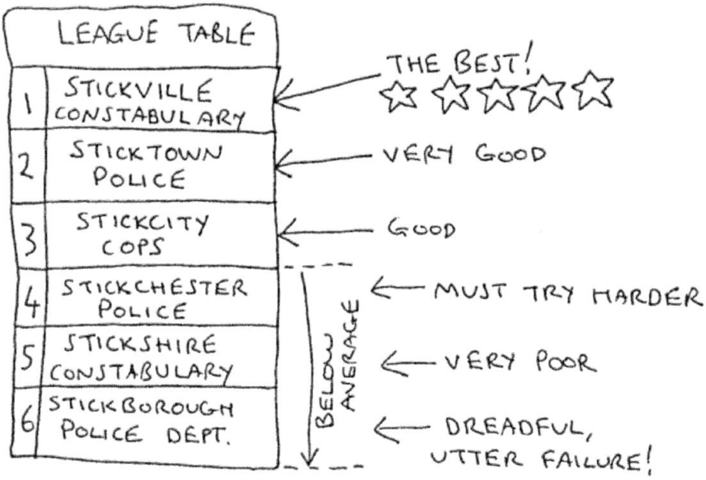
LEAGUE TABLE
1 STICKVILLE CONSTABULARY
2 STICKTOWN POLICE
3 STICKCITY COPS
4 STICKCHESTER POLICE
5 STICKSHIRE CONSTABULARY
6 STICKBOROUGH POLICE DEPT.
THE BEST! ☆☆☆☆☆
VERY GOOD
GOOD
BELOW AVERAGE
MUST TRY HARDER
VERY POOR
DREADFUL, UTTER FAILURE!

A notable problem with league tables is that they are methodologically unsound and notoriously unstable. (This is particularly true of league tables constructed from complex public sector data). Due to statistical considerations I won't inflict upon you here, it is often mathematically impossible to neatly rank institutions in the tidy fashion we are so used to (i.e. one at the top, one at the bottom, and the remainder nicely stacked in between, from best to worst).

You see, in league table world, about half of those ranked end up as 'below average', and someone is always bottom. So not everyone can be above the national average! Why not? Because it's an average!!

What we should be doing is trying to establish if there are *significant differences* between peers, and this can be done very simply in a couple of ways, as demonstrated by Stick Child...

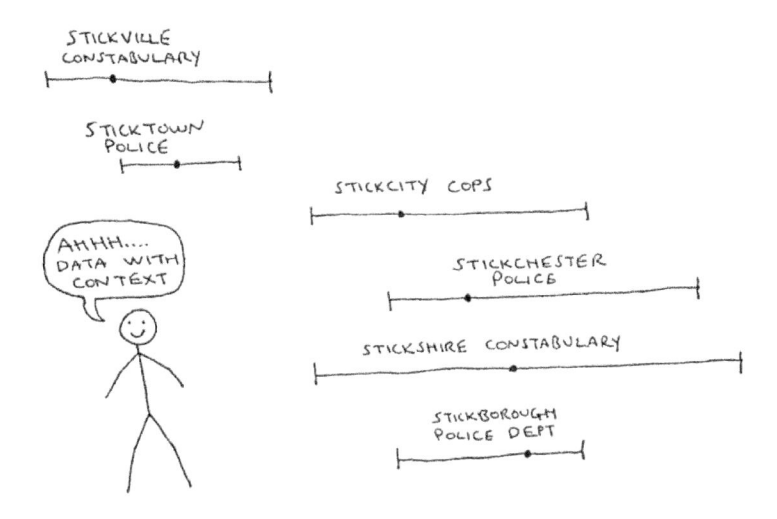

In this first example, the six police forces we saw earlier are assessed against each other, taking into account *confidence intervals* in the data. (Don't worry if you're unfamiliar with the term, just trust me that it's important). As you can see, this tells us that two forces are performing significantly differently to the other four (i.e. there are no overlaps between the two groups).

We can't, however, neatly rank them from 'best' to 'worst', because we can't separate the 'top' two from each other, and we can't separate the other four from each other either.

Here's another way of understanding comparative peer performance in a more contextualised manner:

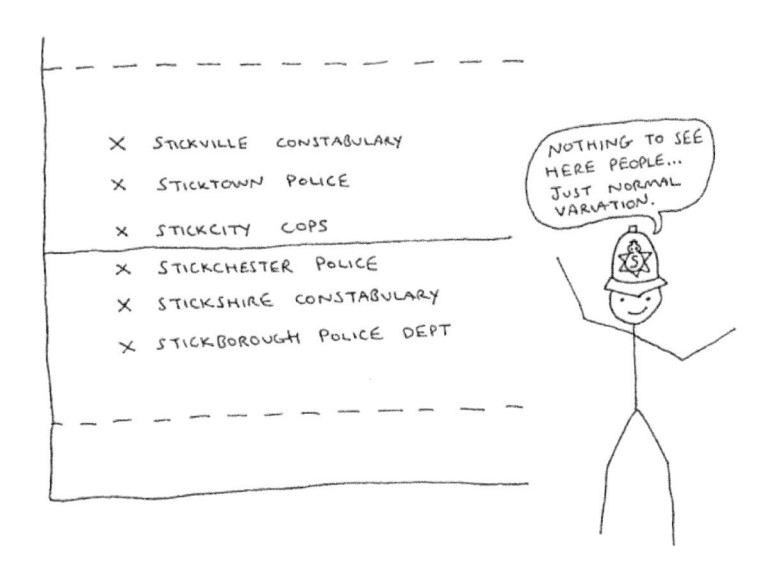

```
|-- -- -- -- -- -- -- -- -- -- --
|
|    X   STICKVILLE  CONSTABULARY       NOTHING TO SEE
|    X   STICKTOWN   POLICE             HERE PEOPLE...
|                                       JUST NORMAL
|    X   STICKCITY   COPS               VARIATION.
|----------------------------------
|    X   STICKCHESTER  POLICE
|    X   STICKSHIRE   CONSTABULARY
|    X   STICKBOROUGH POLICE DEPT
|
|-- -- -- -- -- -- -- -- -- --
|
```

This time we can observe that the six police forces are all within the boundaries of 'normality' (by applying Statistical Process Control methodology). If any of them were outside of the dashed lines we might be concerned that particular force was significantly different from its peers; however, in this case, all six forces are clustered around the mean average (solid horizontal line) and within the range of anticipated performance for the group.

Therefore, there is absolutely no way the forces should be placed in ranked order – they are likely to move positions each time a snapshot is taken because of normal variation, but as long as they stay within the lines (and ideally, improve as a group), it is wrong to judge performance based on apparent position.

You see, when this happens, we encounter the other big problem associated with the league table mindset – concern about someone's position in a league table leads to unfair assumptions about performance, unnecessary 'remedial' activity to address the perceived deficiencies, pressure from management, sanctions, and so on. And all based on something that essentially isn't there. Cue gaming and dysfunctional behaviour! Like clockwork.

And a final thought – if league tables are constructed using crime data, are we even measuring the right thing?

Straight Lines

The other day, Stick Child was playing with his next-door neighbour, Stick Friend. At first, they were having a great time playing with her pet, 'Stick Stick Insect', but soon Stick Child noticed that Stick Friend seemed a bit quieter than usual, so he asked her if anything was wrong.

Stick Friend told Stick Child she felt a bit sad because her teacher had sent home a school report that graded her at level SP3c, when the national average for stick people of her age (8) is level SP3a. The teacher had told Stick Friend that the school would get in trouble if she and her classmates didn't reach their targets by the end of the year.

Stick Child thought that this didn't make any sense – he supposed that the people who decided on these targets must have never heard of that thing called *variation* that he learnt about in his 'red cars project'. Stick Friend hadn't done that project, so Stick Child quickly thought of a way to explain the concept at a level that even an eight-year-old would understand.

He picked up a piece of paper and a pen and drew the following diagram:

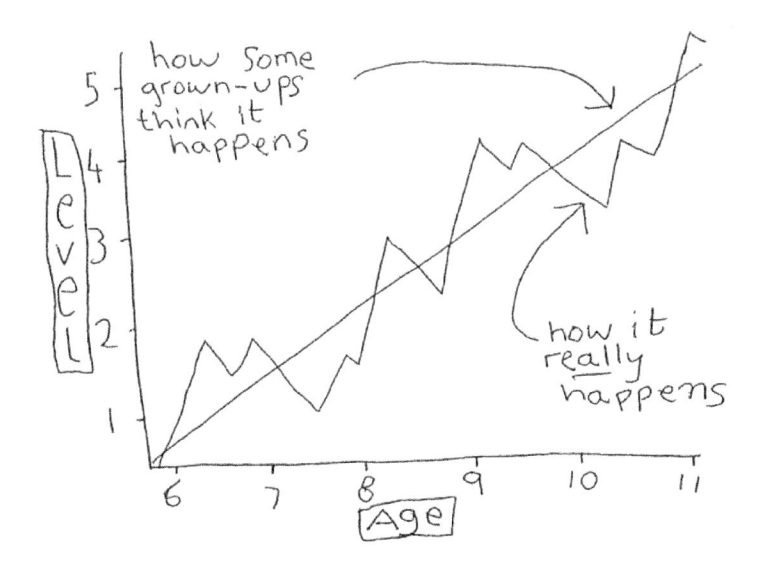

[Hand-drawn diagram showing a graph with "Level" (1-5) on the y-axis and "Age" (6-11) on the x-axis. A straight diagonal line is labelled "how some grown-ups think it happens" and a jagged zig-zag line is labelled "how it really happens".]

Stick Child knew he only had about 15 minutes before dinner, so decided to not even talk about the *dys-function-al behaviour* that numerical targets cause, but just to concentrate on why it is mathematically silly to try and understand performance like this.

Using his drawing, Stick Child explained that some grown-ups believe things happen in straight lines, as in the diagram. In real life however, he pointed out that stick children learn and progress at different rates and in different ways, and showed Stick Friend that even when a child hits their targets by the time they finish 'little stick person school', this progress never ever happens in a perfectly straight line.

As you can see from the drawing, sometimes the child's work level is a bit below average for the stage they're at, and other times it's a bit above average. This happens because of variation and a thing called *regression to the mean*, which is why the zig-zags tend to fluctuate around the average.

This means it's pointless trying to compare isolated fixed points on a scale to the average, a target, a peer, isolated points from the past (binary comparisons give kids nightmares!), or using daily totals or year-to-date figures to see whether performance is 'on track'.

Stick Friend understood this concept straight away and felt much happier. The friends then played with Stick Insect some more, before Stick Child went home for his dinner.

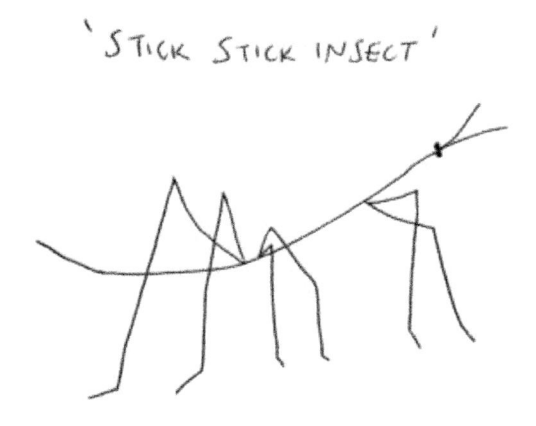

'STICK STICK INSECT'

It took Stick Friend about five minutes to get her head around this stuff.

Even Stick Stick Insect understood most of it.

At home that evening, Stick Child's Daddy told him about some research that was done in the old days (1973). It involved two clever people called Daniel Kahneman and Amos Tversky, who discovered some flight instructors believed that praising trainee pilots after a smooth landing was a bad idea because they sometimes seemed to be worse the next time they tried.

The flight instructors also believed that telling the pilots off for a poor landing helped to make them better, because they often performed smoother landings after being shouted at. The sad thing was that the pilots were actually getting better and better all the time – just not in a straight line – yet because the instructors didn't understand variation or regression to the mean, they believed the best way to help them improve was to get angry with them when they were 'failing'.

If you wished, you could draw a similar diagram to Stick Child's, which shows gradual improvement of trainee pilots. (Or one that shows crime decreasing. Or profits going up. Or people living longer. Or unemployment going down. Or stock market shares increasing. Or anything else that improves or worsens over time).

As Stick Child points out – none of these things ever happen in a straight line. Hopefully, this illustrates why comparing performance (or any a fixed point) against a straight line leads to muddled perceptions, impaired decision-making and panicked reactions such as:

"We can only afford 'X' amount of 'Y' per day, otherwise we'll miss the target!"

Don't do it!

Maths Class

Here's Stick Teacher. Today Stick Teacher is going to run through a few sums with the Stick Children. Adults might find his case studies useful too. Stick Teacher is going to demonstrate how to save money whilst providing a better service – what's not to like?

To do this, he'll use the example of a generic public sector call centre (police / ambulance / fire / tax office / housing department / other*).

*DELETE AS APPLICABLE.

The idea that these call centres save money seems to be based on the premise that if you put a lot of people in a central location and give them a specific function that forms part of the overall service provided, it's cheaper.

Let's try and understand how this concept works, using characters that Stick Teacher has invented to help explain things to the Stick Children...

Here's Employee 1.

Employee 1 is an enthusiastic call taker and a hard worker, who always assists the public the very best he can with his level of training and experience.

EMPLOYEE 1

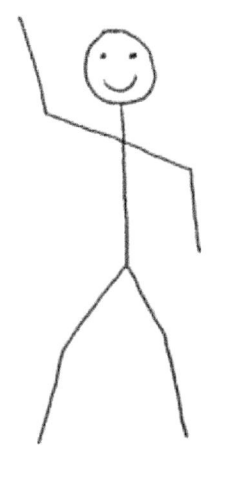

And this is Employee 2. She is also enthusiastic and hard-working, but more senior, more highly trained and experienced; plus, she is empowered by the organisation to make decisions about stuff.

Here we go then...

Case Study: Option One

For this example, Employee 1 answers a call, asks basic details and creates an electronic record. He is paid 10 Stick Coins per hour (this is the currency in Stick Land) and spends 15 minutes dealing with the call.

Time elapsed so far = 15 minutes.

Total cost so far = 2.50 Stick Coins.

Employee 1 then forwards the electronic record to Employee 2; being more senior, more highly trained and experienced, she is paid 20 Stick Coins per hour. Her role is to review the electronic records, identify any additional actions and make a decision about what to do.

On this occasion, she identifies that Employee 1 has covered most of the basics, but thinks it would be helpful to ask a few more questions and do some background checks before a resource is allocated to deal with the case, so she details these requirements on the electronic record and returns it to Employee 1 to complete.

She spends 15 minutes doing this (costing a further 5 Stick Coins).

Time elapsed so far = 30 minutes.

Total cost so far = 7.50 Stick Coins.

Employee 1 then completes these tasks and sends the case to the appropriate resource. This takes another 15 minutes, costing another 2.50 Stick Coins.

Total time elapsed = 45 minutes

Call rate per hour = 1.33

Total cost = 10 Stick Coins

So, that's the traditional call centre model then.

Case Study: Option Two

An alternative approach would be put Employee 2 at the point of contact with service users, where she can maximise her skills and experience to do a more thorough job from the outset, thereby negating the requirement to pass the job backwards and forwards for review and remedial actions. Due to her enhanced ability, she is able to deal with the entire case in 15 minutes.

Total time elapsed = 15 minutes

Call rate per hour = 4

Total cost = 5 Stick Coins

So, although it costs twice as much to employ her, the job gets done more quickly and effectively. Oh, and the whole process costs half as much as in Option One.

Case Study: Option Three

But perhaps your organisation wouldn't want to use a raft of 'Employee 2s' at a higher rate of pay, so a third option could be to employ Employee 3, who is just as enthusiastic and hard-working as his colleagues. (There is no file picture of Employee 3, so you'll have to imagine what he looks like).

Employee 3 is quite capable of handling 95% of calls without assistance; he is more highly trained than Employee 1, but isn't trained to the highest level of specialism, like Employee 2. This means he is paid 16 Stick Coins per hour. He is able to deal with most cases to the same level as Employee 2, and at the same rate. Therefore, he deals with this call in 15 minutes, costing 4 Stick Coins.

Total time elapsed = 15 minutes

Call rate per hour = 4

Total cost = 4 Stick Coins

On those few occasions where Employee 2's specialist training is required to make decisions on the most complex cases, this model would allow for a small number of such experts to be available, commensurate with the demand for their enhanced skills.

So, this model is also faster and costs much less than the traditional call centre model; the only consideration is there will be a handful of occasions where some calls need to be passed to Employee 2 to complete. If the cost / benefit implications of this model are acceptable, then this configuration could be the most cost-effective of all three.

Stick Teacher's Conclusions

Therefore, the result of today's lesson for the Stick Children is that conventional wisdom about things like centralised functions is not always that wise. Whichever way you look at it, Option One is actually the slowest and most expensive to operate; Option Two is the ideal model from the caller's perspective, and Option Three is probably the most cost-effective and suitable configuration for the real world.

The illusion of savings under Option One comes about because of the focus on cost-per-operator, without understanding end-to-end flow or whether purpose is achieved. It builds in waste, unnecessary handovers, disempowers staff, creates delays and COSTS MORE, whilst providing a WORSE service!

Therefore, maybe more people should try one of the other options instead.

Stick Child's Guessing Game

Stick Child and his friends sometimes play a game where they take turns to throw dice and everyone tries to guess the number that will come up. It's an enjoyable game, but the stick children know it's just a bit of fun – even when one of them guesses the number correctly they know it's luck, because when two dice are thrown, the total could be any number between two and twelve. None of the children really believe they had genuinely predicted the number, or that a particular number came up because of how the dice were thrown.

One day, Stick Child and his friends were playing the guessing game, when along walked Stick Cop. Now, the 'Daily Stick' newspaper may have you believe that most stick cops would treat what the children were doing as 'anti-social behaviour', but really, most of them are not like that at all. Stick Cop just wanted to say hello to the children and make sure they were safe and enjoying themselves.

After Stick Cop had played a couple of rounds of the guessing game with the stick children, Stick Child told him about his 'straight lines' theory. Stick Cop thought it was fascinating because he could see how it applied to his line of work. You see, Stick Cop works with some really clever people called 'The Stick Analysts', and although they sound like a 1960s rock band, they are actually a group of very bright folk who understand numbers and use their knowledge to try and help their bosses make good decisions.

One of the things The Stick Analysts do is try to work out what might happen with things like crime rates. They throw lots of numbers into a big machine and it produces charts like the ones Stick Child draws. Sometimes the machine tells them that crime might be going up or down over time, and this makes it possible to predict (to an extent) where crime rates might be heading.

The Stick Analysts know, however, that accurate prediction is dependent upon on the overall crime rate trajectory remaining the same as it was at the point when they threw the numbers into the machine. Also, even if it continues to increase or decrease at exactly the same rate, even the cleverest of Stick Analysts could only say that the future crime rate could be anticipated to fall within a certain *range*. This is just like saying that the dice will produce a number somewhere between two and twelve on each throw.

Unfortunately, what sometimes happens is a 'Mystery Targets Monster' gets hold of the good work done by The Stick Analysts and either swaps it for some indecipherable twoddle based on *binary comparisons*, or worse still, decides that it's possible to choose one of those numbers somewhere within the predicted range and turn it into a target. This is because the Mystery Targets Monster refuses to listen to the experts and thinks it knows better.

The Mystery Targets Monster earned its 'mysterious' qualification at college because often no one seems to know who put the targets in, or why. It's a very cunning, elusive, but fundamentally confused (and grubby) creature that exists in a fantasy world where evidence about the dysfunctional effects of numerical targets is countered by simply being ignored.

Anyway, once the Mystery Targets Monster has ruined the report that The Stick Analysts have produced, it emits a shrill giggle then runs back to its secret lair. The report then goes to the big police bosses who try to do their best with what they've been given.

Meanwhile, the Mystery Targets Monster plays the dice guessing game by itself, becoming increasingly angry because its predicted number doesn't come up every time, like it thinks it should. Whenever its predicted number fails to materialise, the Mystery Targets Monster goes out and roars unintelligibly at the first thing it sees, thinking that this will make the dice behave differently next time.

It adopts the same approach with target setting, which of course is also a complete guessing game.

The Mystery Targets Monster just doesn't get it at all!

Fortunately, Stick Child and his pals do. So do The Stick Analysts. And Stick Cop.

Hopefully you do too.

Three Different Things

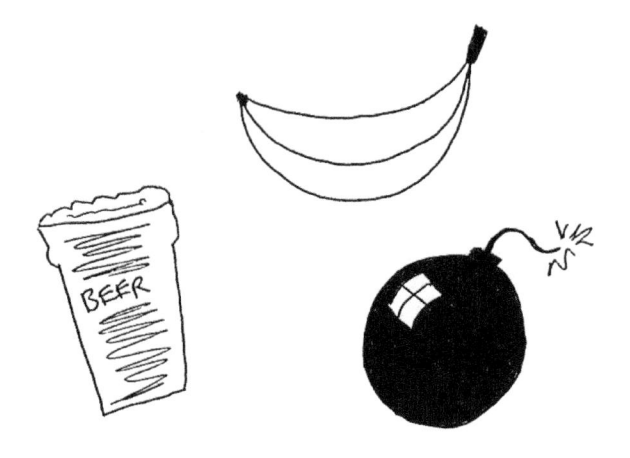

This follows on from 'Spot The Difference' as it explores related concepts.

Okay, so you've recognised that the banana, beer and cartoon bomb are three different things. Are you as confident that you could differentiate between 'priorities', 'measures' and 'numerical targets' though?

I ask because these are also *three different things*, yet they are routinely conflated with each other; this leads to mental stumbling blocks for those trying to move beyond the targets culture in performance management.

So, to break it down…

Priorities are the things considered important. They are what the organisation places value upon. They should reflect the aim (or aims) of the system. They focus attention, direction, effort and activity. Having no priorities is bad, because it means the system is directionless.

But they're NOT numerical targets!

Measures are just the bits of quantitative and qualitative information that we use to establish whether we are attaining priorities. Measures are really important, because if we use the right measures in the right way, we can understand what is happening within the system and identify opportunities to improve. The data from the measures help us make better decisions. Better decisions lead to better outcomes. Having no measures is bad, because without them, we can't understand how the system is performing.

But they're NOT numerical targets!

Numerical Targets are the random aspirational numbers that human beings invent in their heads because they think they need them to make people do a good job. Target setters aren't necessarily bad people, but they forget some important points, like these:

- Numerical targets are arbitrary.
- Numerical targets do not provide a method or capacity for achieving priorities.
- No numerical target is immune from causing dysfunctional behaviour.

But they're NOT priorities or measures!

Therefore, I argue that if you're clear about your priorities and use appropriate measures, you've got what you need. The numerical targets simply don't need to be there at all.

They're irrelevant and often make performance *worse*. So why have them at all?

Here's an example. It should be easy to see that the priorities, measures and numerical targets in this table are *three different things*. Now, just imagine that the numerical targets aren't there. What you're left with is the useful stuff – *priorities* and *measures*.

But they're NOT numerical targets!

Priority	Measures	Numerical Target
Tackle crime	• Data about crime rates • Data about detected crime • Data about the factors that led to crimes being solved (e.g. prompt attendance, forensic results, witness enquiries, CCTV evidence) • Data about police resourcing • Data about deployment times • Lots of other stuff	Errrm...*puts finger in the air*... • Reduce crime by 5% • Detect 20% of crime • Answer non-emergency calls within 30 seconds, 90% of the time

STICK CHILD SAYS...

PRIORITIES AND MEASURES ARE IMPORTANT, BUT THEY'RE NOT NUMERICAL TARGETS!

Stick Child Tries to Buy Milk

Stick Child is a healthy little chappie and he loves a nice cold drink of milk at break time. His usual routine is to go to the hatch in the school dinner hall when the bell rings for morning break, where he hands over his money and collects a nice cold drink of milk. Then he goes out to play with his friends.

Today, however, things were different – the milk counter was closed because the school had adopted a new system for break time milk sales. When Stick Child went into the school hall, he saw a table with a telephone on it and a sign that read, *'Milk-Related Transactions Centre'*

Stick Child dialled the number listed in some instructions that were on the table, put the phone handset to his ear, and waited to see what would happen...

Then, instead of a human saying "Hello Stick Child, how are you today?" as usual, he encountered an automated voice that said:

"Welcome to our new and more efficient way of dealing with milk-related transactions. Please select from the list of available options".

Stick Child thought this was odd, but listened to the options, which were:

- *"Press ONE if you wish to discuss your milk account".*

- *"Press TWO for information about how much milk you've used so far this term".*

- *"Press THREE if you would like to upgrade to our premier milk account, or to hear about a range of special offers".*

Stick Child waited for Option FOUR, which he hoped might be "Speak to a human being", or "Buy some milk", but it never came. This confused him, so he chose Option ONE, which he supposed was the least inaccurate of all the choices, although he didn't really want to *discuss* his milk account – he just wanted some milk. To drink.

Upon pressing Option ONE, Stick Child was immediately advised by the automated voice that it would be better for everyone if he just went and used the internet in future. Then it told him to be sure to check out 'our new range of sweets, crisps and chocolates'. Stick Child wasn't bothered about any of those things though – he just wanted to buy some milk!

After these messages, Stick Child was put on hold for a few minutes, whilst the phone played Bruno Mars records into his ear. Every so often, Bruno's velvet tones were interrupted by another robotic voice that advised:

"Your call is important to us and one of our operators will be with you to deal with your query as soon as possible".

After a while, another automated voice announced:

"We are experiencing unusually high call volumes at this time. You may wish to call back later or use our online milk information service".

Stick Child thought it was odd that whoever had designed the new system hadn't anticipated milk-related demand would peak at break time.

Anyway, he continued to hold, until eventually a human answered and politely informed him that he had come through to the wrong department and would have to dial the number again. This human tried to be helpful, advising Stick Child that he would need to choose Option TWO, then sub-menu Option NINE, followed by sub-sub-menu Option FORTY SIX, then ask for 'DAVE'.

At that point, the end-of-break bell rang and poor Stick Child had to return to class, without any milk. Stick Child was disappointed. He thinks this new system is rubbish and that the old way of buying milk at break time was better for lots of reasons.

Postscript

In case you're wondering what would have happened if Stick Child had managed to speak to the right person / voice recognition entity on the phone, then apparently under this new regime he would be allocated a unique reference number, which he must take to a new counter at the opposite end of the school.

There, his reference code will be checked and he will be given a token, before being sent to a third counter somewhere else, where he will hand over the token and collect his milk. The whole process is subject to rigorous service level standards at each stage and audited under a tough inspection regime, of course.

On Purpose

This machine is a Purpose Obfuscation O-meter. (Work out the acronym for yourself).

I know you love my drawings.

A lot of organisations use these devices. This is how they work:

A customer or service user leans towards the 'In' funnel on the left hand side of the machine and states what he or she requires from the system. The machine scrambles the soundwaves into what it thinks is a pretty good interpretation of what the customer or service user has said. It then spits out its version of what it thinks the system's *purpose* is into the 'Out' basket, giving the frontline workers instructions on what to do.

The machine is very versatile and can be utilised in many organisational settings, both in the public and private sectors. Let's see it in action...

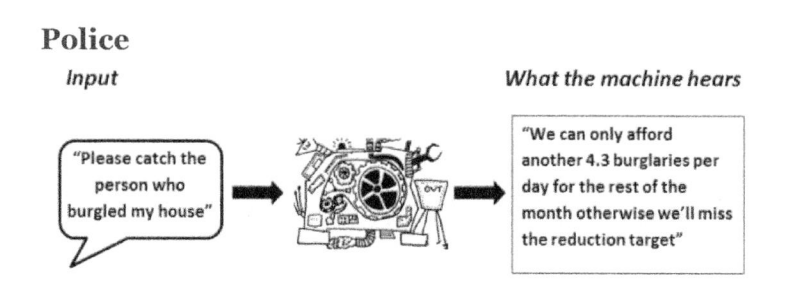

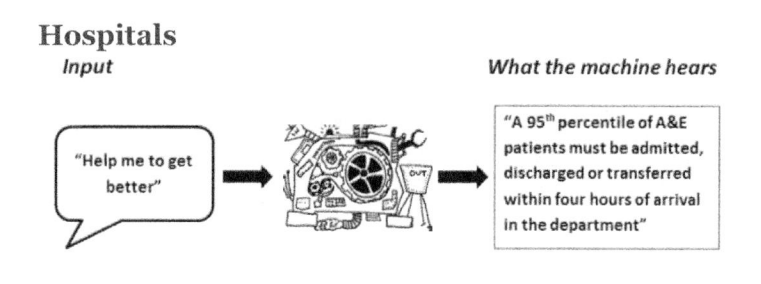

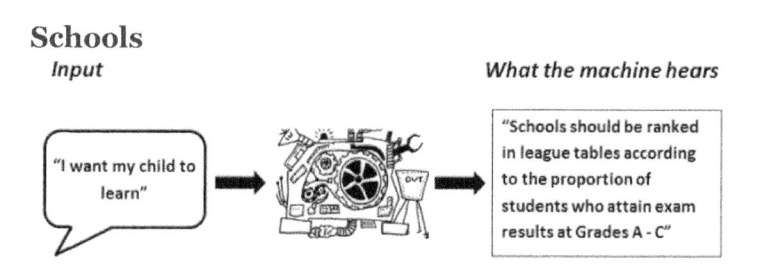

Police

Input   *What the machine hears*

"Please catch the person who burgled my house"

→

"We can only afford another 4.3 burglaries per day for the rest of the month otherwise we'll miss the reduction target"

Hospitals

Input   *What the machine hears*

"Help me to get better"

→

"A 95th percentile of A&E patients must be admitted, discharged or transferred within four hours of arrival in the department"

Schools

Input   *What the machine hears*

"I want my child to learn"

→

"Schools should be ranked in league tables according to the proportion of students who attain exam results at Grades A - C"

Sales
Input *What the machine hears*

"I'd like to buy some stuff" → [machine] → "Make the sale now and book it before the end of the quarter even though it's not in stock. The customer can have it in six weeks"

Call Centres
Input *What the machine hears*

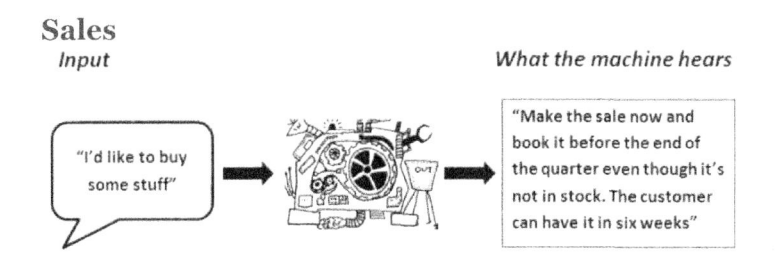

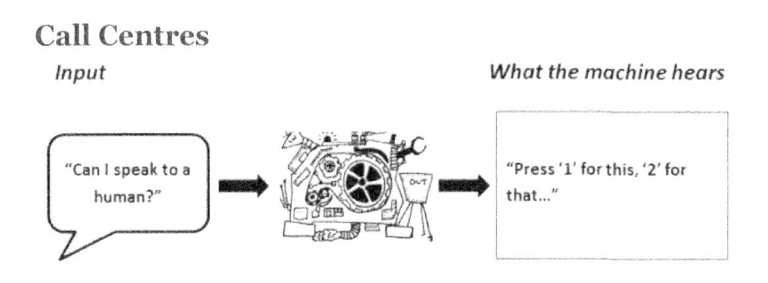

"Can I speak to a human?" → [machine] → "Press '1' for this, '2' for that..."

As you can see, the machine is pretty rubbish and although the people who installed it were well-intentioned, their best efforts have resulted in something that actually distorts true purpose, as defined by the customer or service user.

This causes the frontline workers to behave differently, in order to meet the new *de facto* purpose generated by the machine. Effort is then focused on this pseudo purpose, as it has now inadvertently supplanted the real purpose of the system.

Workers can become very adept at meeting the machine's definition of 'purpose', whilst simultaneously failing to attain the real purpose, which has now been obfuscated (the machine does what it says on the tin). Sometimes, the workers still manage to meet true purpose, but fail to achieve what the machine *thinks* is the system's purpose. This causes them to get in trouble.

It also means that managers have to initiate a lot of audit and inspection to ensure that the machine is satisfied. Unfortunately this costs a lot of time, money and effort. It also makes the workers and customers or service users feel fed up.

The solution is simple:

If your organisation uses one of these machines, just turn it off and LISTEN to what your customers or service users are asking for. Then, design the front end of your organisation to handle predictable demand. That way, you end up with a responsive system that is geared towards meeting its *true purpose*, which is no longer obfuscated by one of these silly machines.

Easy isn't it?

The alternative is P.O.O.

The People vs The System

In the red corner: *"People are our greatest asset"*.

In the blue corner: *"94% of performance comes from the system; 6% from the people"*.

Which is better? There's only one way to find out...

FIGHT!!!

Or maybe not.

You see, both corners have merit. The people in any system are really important, and yes, they are part of the system. But so are other system conditions, such as organisational climate, structures, norms, relationships, interdependencies, culture, networks, informal and formal practices, processes, internal and external influences, environmental factors, and many more.

Let's not get hung up on what the system is, where its boundaries are, which bits overlap with other systems, where sub-systems are positioned and so on. So much of this is impossible to define. Let's not try and establish the percentage split between 'people' and 'system' when it comes to trying to understand where the greatest opportunities for performance come from.

In complex public service settings such as policing, it is difficult enough to define and measure outcomes, let alone figure out which bit contributed towards achieving them, or what proportion came from the people.

My view is that all those systems conditions contribute towards achieving the purpose of the system, including of course, the people. The two aren't really in different corners.

BUT...

The people can only operate within the constraints of the other system conditions. This multitude of system conditions must be conducive to enabling the people to achieve their full potential. Otherwise it's like putting a world-class acrobat in one of those heavy old diving suits, and expecting them to perform well...

What's Your Poison?

Imagine you've been out to a restaurant for a meal and when you get home, you experience agonising stomach cramps, blurred vision and other symptoms too horrible to describe here.

When you're well enough to leave the house, you return to the restaurant to complain. The manager makes some enquiries in the kitchen, then informs you that the cook had added a few drops of poison to your food.

The cook meant well though; after all, he'd been adding poison to customers' meals for a while and no one had died.

Anyway, the manager is really sorry that you've had a bad experience. He admits he's heard that poison can sometimes cause adverse effects, so as a gesture of goodwill he suggests the following options to prevent future poisonings:

1. The chef could be more careful about the way he mixes the poison into the food. Maybe it's the way the chef is pouring it that's the problem, rather than the actual poison.

2. He could use less poison. Or maybe water it down a bit. This way, the effects wouldn't be as bad.

3. Alternatively, he could try using different types of poison. Maybe it's just that particular type of poison which is the problem.

In any case, the manager absolutely refuses to stop using poison – He laments, "What alternative is there to the use of poison?"

STOP!

Well that's all just a bit silly isn't it? Who'd knowingly put poison in food, thinking it would improve it? Furthermore, who'd honestly believe those 'options' for preventing future poisonings would actually make a difference?

Number 1 assumes it's a people problem and that applying the same poison in a slightly different manner will achieve different results. (Definition of madness, anyone?)

Number 2 is what John Seddon calls, "Doing less of the wrong thing", or what Russ Ackoff says is, "Doing the wrong thing righter".

Number 3 is just a desperate denial that the poison could ever possibly be the problem. "Hey folks, it must have been the *wrong type* of poison!" Of course. Let's go and poison people with slightly different strains instead! Genius.

And as for the manager's pitiful concerns about what they'd be left with if they removed the poison from the recipe... well I'll tell you. *No poison in your food.*

Can you see where this is going yet? You might have guessed there's a 'hidden' meaning to this story. Let's recap. It's...

- Something known to cause adverse, yet unintended effects when introduced into the equation.

- Something that some managers cling to because they can't see what the alternatives might be.

- Something whose entirely predictable consequences are reacted to as in the 'options' above, rather than by addressing the root cause – the poison itself.

Still unsure?

Then go back and read the post again, but replace the word *poison* with *numerical targets*.

Lose Weight with Systems Thinking

One of the key tenets of systems thinking is understanding *variation*. Deming said:

"Life is variation. Variation there will always be, between people, in output, in service, in product".

This applies to weight loss as much as everything else. People who are trying to lose weight often become frustrated that despite their best efforts, the scales mock them, telling them they haven't lost any weight since they weighed themselves yesterday, or worse still, they have *gained* a pound or two.

This can also apply when comparing one's weight to this time last week, or any other single point in time.

That's the problem, you see – making a comparison to one other solitary value is meaningless. This is the case for a couple of reasons:

1. You are making a simplistic *binary comparison* against a moving variable that merely captures an arbitrary point in the past.

2. The comparison does not take into account external factors that affect the data. For example, in weight loss terms, several factors can influence what the scales tell you, such as the time of day you weigh yourself, your body's degree of water retention at that moment in time, or how recently you have eaten.

Binary comparisons are meaningless and tell us nothing. Here's what one looks like on a chart:

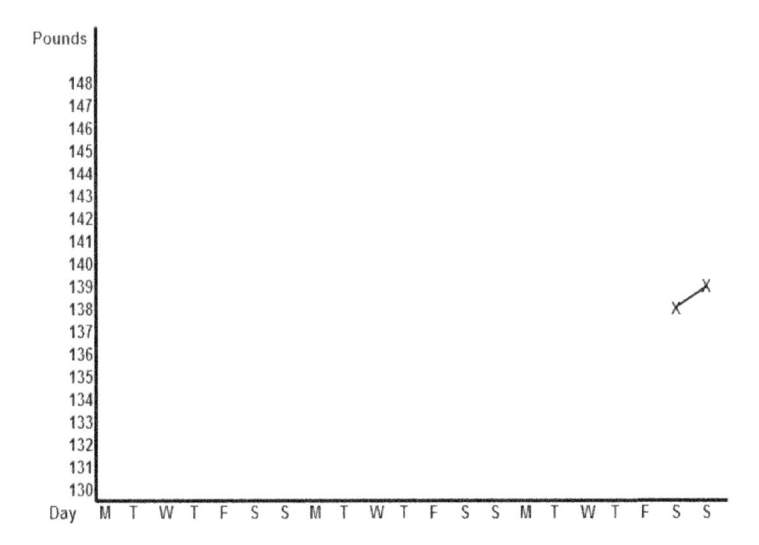

Pants, isn't it?

Instead, to establish whether there are any real trends in a data set, a better way is to plot several data points on a control chart, such as in the one below:

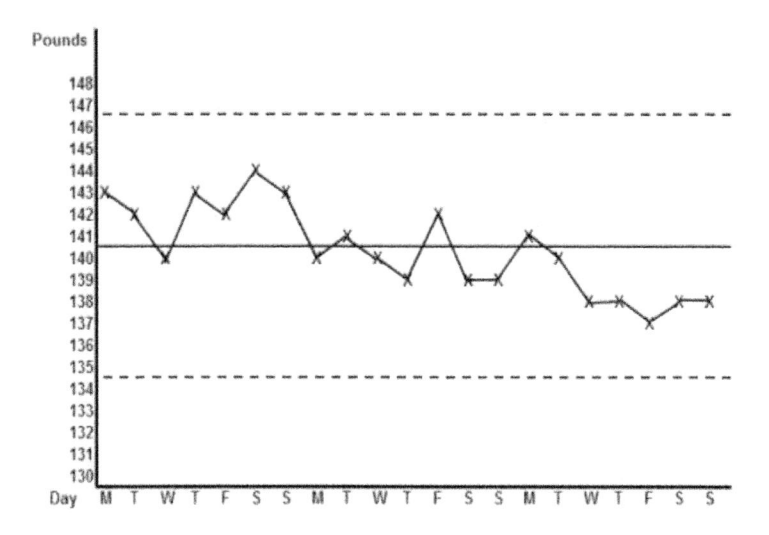

Basically, if the data points don't fall outside of the control limits (the dashed lines), or form any of a handful of specific patterns that I won't bore you with, then what you see is *normal variation*.

Normal variation is normal!! Sometimes the numbers go up; sometimes they go down. There is always a degree of fluctuation in anything – the number of red cars that drive past per hour, the crime rate, your weight.

Here it is clear to see that the person to whom the data pertain has experienced a steady rate of weight loss over a three week period. But let's go back to the traditional binary comparison method that people tend to use when trying to establish if they are losing weight. For the first couple of days our subject would be overjoyed to discover that their weight loss programme appears to be working. Unfortunately, this would be followed by shock and disappointment that he or she suddenly *gained* three pounds! Whaaat??!!

Worst of all, on the sixth day of the programme, the scales indicate the person is two pounds heavier than the previous day and a pound heavier than when they started!! How cruel. Imagine their sense of frustration and disappointment. "Stupid scales!" "Waste of time!" "The diet's not working!" Recognise any of this?

Over the next few days, our subject experiences a loss of a few more pounds and would probably feel a bit happier. Then, on the second Friday of the programme, he or she records a 'sudden' and 'massive' weight gain of three pounds...ARRRGGHHH!!

And so it continues. Some days the scales bring good news; other days frustration, purely based on whether the numbers are higher or lower than the previous day, or as compared to any other given single point in the past, such as 'this time last week'.

This demonstrates why this method of comparing data is fundamentally flawed. A steady and identifiable trend of weight loss becomes obscured by honing in on just two readings. People become unhappy and wonder what they are doing wrong. The answer is probably nothing. It's just normal variation, so stop worrying about it. In the same way, those trying to lose weight feel elated when the scales show an apparent decrease.

So don't fool yourself – if you're comparing your weight to yesterday the 'decrease' is just probably normal variation again. In the same way – should you experience a 'sudden' or 'massive' increase, remember that it's neither sudden nor massive. Making a judgment on two data points is always unsound. Don't do it!

Even if you don't know how to construct a proper control chart, just plot your weight loss data on any old chart over time. You will see ups and downs. That's normal. Hopefully, over time, if you are doing the right things to lose weight, you will see a steady reduction. This is impossible to see when using the binary comparison approach.

The Weather Man

Sometimes when Stick Child and his friends are out playing, they see an old man walking his dog. They call this man 'The Weather Man', because he always asks the stick children to help him predict the weather. He asks the children to pick a pebble from the nearby stream, then he looks at it carefully, before declaring whether tomorrow's weather will be sunny or rainy, hot or cold, windy or calm.

The stick children like the old man, but think his weather forecasting antics are rather odd and amusing, because he's not usually right. He thinks that if the pebble is larger or smaller, a different colour or a different shape than the one yesterday, this enables him to predict what tomorrow's weather will be like. Often they see him walking his dog in his T-shirt and Bermuda shorts in torrential rain, or sweltering in a thick duffle coat on a scorching hot day because he got it wrong again.

One day, the stick children asked the old man why he thought he could predict the weather by comparing pebbles and he told them it was because he'd always done it that way. He also said that it must be a good indicator of forthcoming weather patterns because sometimes his predictions had actually been correct.

The stick children felt a bit sorry for him because he believed in what he was doing, but they all knew that his method was no good. Then one of them had an idea – her Mummy had just bought a new television and she didn't know what to do with the old one. The stick children had a meeting (not like the ones grown-ups have, which go on for several hours) and after two minutes they decided to ask the old man if he wanted the old television, so he could watch real weather forecasts.

Next time they saw the old man, they told him about their plan and he was really excited, because he'd never owned a television before. That afternoon, the stick children took the television round to his house and set it up. They showed him how to find the weather forecast and explained how weather experts use *real science* for predicting what the weather will be like.

The old man was very impressed and thanked the stick children for their thoughtfulness. Now he knows there is a better way to understand and forecast the weather than by trying to use pebbles from the stream, which means he no longer gets caught in downpours in his Bermuda shorts. After realising this, he couldn't believe anyone would ever try and use pebbles at all.

Stick Child's Thought of the Day

For anyone who knows Stick Child, you'll probably have already figured out that the weather analogy is all about understanding measures properly.

The stones represent *binary comparisons* (i.e. a completely useless 'method' prone to giving wrong signals) whilst the proper weather forecast reflects the use of *control charts* and associated scientific methods for understanding data properly. Better methods of understanding data lead to better choices – what's not to like?

Bear in mind that neither control charts nor television weather reports are always 100% accurate, but they use *real science*, so they're a whole lot better than pulling pebbles out of a stream.

If the old man was prepared to change his method to something that actually works, so can you.

Avoidable Harm

A few years ago the National Health Service had a high-profile campaign called 'Sign up for Safety", which aimed to reduce *avoidable harm* in the NHS. Now, avoidable harm is clearly something worth tackling. The sticking point for me was that they chose a numerical target to reduce avoidable harm by 50%.

What I can't understand is why anyone would aim to reduce AVOIDABLE harm by 50% – if it's avoidable, we should avoid it! Not just some of it. Why would you want to be 'half-safe'?

It's like deliberately planning to retain the other 50% of harm! Which, of course, sounds silly – because it IS silly. There's a lot that's silly (and harmful) about such targets, such as the assumption that a target is necessary to make people want to reduce harm in the first place. If they know that reducing harm is important (i.e. a *priority*), then the target is irrelevant.

It might even be possible to measure some types of harm reduction, so that's good too, because then you have *measures* to help you understand how your harm reduction efforts are going. The target is still irrelevant though.

Anyway, why is the target 50%? How was this determined? Why not 55%, or 70%, or 81.648%? If it was set at 50% because it was deemed attainable, then what's the point of the target, because you're going to attain it anyway, right?

File photo: Stick Child smashing up some arbitrary numerical targets

Why is a 49.999% reduction a failure, whereas a 50.001% reduction a success? These invisible dividing lines between 'good' and 'bad' simply don't exist in the real world. If you could reduce more harm than 50% then you would, wouldn't you? If so, the target is irrelevant. If you wouldn't, then why not?

How about if you reduced all the harm you possibly could, but this only amounted to 35% less harm? Have you failed? Why? What about if you had it within your gift to reduce harm by around 80-90%, but only reduced it by 55%? You've exceeded the target, but is this good?

Then there's the stuff about *method*. How does a numerical target set at any level help you identify and address harm reduction opportunities? It doesn't, because *targets don't provide a method.*

Surely it's better to aim for 100% (i.e. perfection) and see what can be achieved. You'd then measure, learn and improve as you go along. Yes, in many domains (such as harm or crime reduction) it may not ultimately be possible to completely eradicate the object of your reduction efforts, but this shouldn't stop anyone from trying.

Let me give you a few examples using the Stick People, to try and demonstrate why numerical targets like the 50% target for avoidable harm are pointless (not to mention arbitrary and prone to causing dysfunctional behaviour).

Here's Stick Doctor. Today, Stick Doctor encountered two opportunities to reduce harm in her hospital. Guess how many she addressed? (Clue: It wasn't one).

This is Stick Cop. Stick Cop currently has four investigations in his in-tray. He's decided to investigate all of them to the best of his ability. Not just two.

Here's Stick Child again. Stick Child saw one opportunity to help a group of under-10s get their heads around some basic performance management concepts. He didn't stop half way through.

Get it now?

If you have a worthwhile priority, just focus on that. Measure your progress, using the right measures in the right way. Learn and improve. You don't need the target.

Reduce avoidable harm by reducing numerical targets!

By 100%.

A Tale of Two Kings

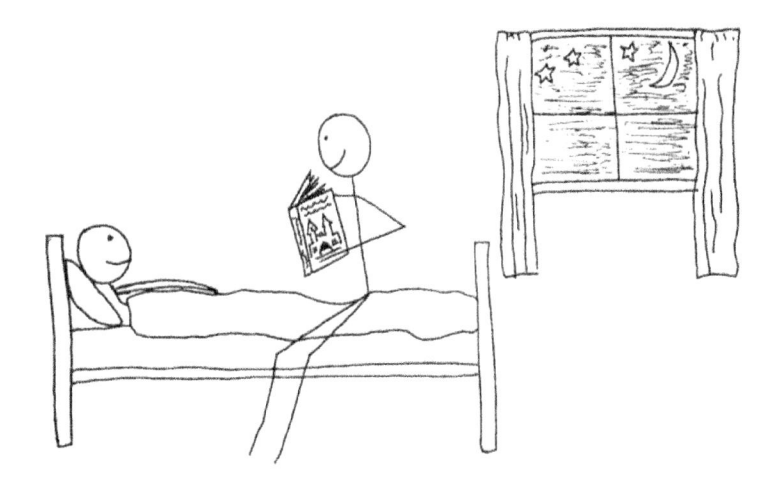

At bedtime, Stick Child's Daddy often reads his son a story from his favourite story book, "Medieval Stories from Stick Kingdom with an Inevitable Systems Thinking Moral". One recent story they particularly enjoyed was called "A Tale of Two Kings", which went a bit like this...

Once upon a time, many years ago, the King of Stick Kingdom decided to commission artwork to decorate his palace, so he secured the services of the greatest artist in the land – Stick Artist. He asked Stick Artist to paint him the most wonderful painting she could imagine. Stick Artist was up for the challenge and immediately fetched out her canvas, easel, brushes and paints.

But then...just as Stick Artist was about to begin her masterpiece, Stick King said, "Oh, can you make sure you put some rhinos in the picture? I like rhinos". Stick Artist said, "No problem, Stick King", and began to paint.

Then Stick King stopped her again and said, "Oh, by the way, I really like the colour purple, so would you make sure there's lots of purple in the picture?" "Okay, Stick King", said Stick Artist. After a few minutes, Stick King announced, "Oh, and I'd like the picture to be circular". Stick Artist sighed quietly, doffed her beret, then began to cut her canvass into a circle.

This went on - spaceships, explosions, dinosaurs, zig-zags, mountains, more purple, hold the brush with your left hand, a little pink, some clouds, every third brush stroke to be 93.7 degrees adjacent to the previous one, and bananas. Stick Artist did as she was told, despite her mounting frustration (as she was the greatest artist in the land), until finally the picture was ready.

"Aggghhh – it's an abomination!!" yelled the Stick King as the incoherent travesty of a painting was unveiled. "It's a crime against art!" he raged.

Stick Artist took the hint and ran away very quickly before she could be imprisoned. She thought it was a bit rich that the Stick King had blamed her for the mess that ensued after being so prescriptive with his daft ideas, especially as he wasn't an artist himself.

Anyway, Stick Artist escaped to a neighbouring land, where the Stick Emperor soon heard of her reputation and commissioned her to paint him a painting for his palace. Stick Artist accepted the task, listened to Stick Emperor's general ideas about what he wanted, then produced the greatest piece of art that had ever been seen in Stick Land.

This merrie tayle goes to show that you get better results out of people who know their craft if you give them broad direction, rather than interfere and micromanage what they do. If only Stick King had been able to visit the future when this was more widely known.

Concepts like 'Commander's Intent' (where a clear aim is communicated by a military leader, whilst affording flexibility and autonomy to subordinates to develop their own tactics) were unknown in medieval Stick Kingdoms. Notions such as workers being intrinsically motivated by a sense of autonomy, mastery and purpose were also unheard of by Stick Kings hundreds of years ago.

The good news for us today is that this stuff *is* known.

Comfort Blanket

When Stick Child was younger, he had a little comfort blanket. Here he is with it, dreaming about smashing up some arbitrary numerical targets. (That's supposed to be the moon in the window by the way – not a banana).

Stick Child believed that his comfort blanket had magical powers – it kept monsters away at night and helped him sleep soundly. It felt soft and warm, so if he was ever sad he would hold it against the side of his face. It was familiar and reassuring.

Some adults adopt a similar approach.

Despite evidence that binary comparisons are incapable of telling us anything about trends or trajectories, are prone to causing unwarranted assumptions, consistently impair decision making and lead to unnecessary action as a direct result, some adults still cling to them like a comfort blanket. (The same applies to numerical targets and league tables).

In case of any confusion, here's a simple guide:

TWO TYPES OF COMFORT BLANKET

✓ OKAY FOR CHILDREN

FEB 22	FEB 23	
28%	29%	↑
33%	28%	↓
25%	24%	↓
31%	32%	↑
30%	29%	↓

✗ NEVER OKAY

So, to conclude: binary comparisons do not have magical powers and any 'reassurance' they appear to provide is false.

Comfort blankets can be great for children, but adults need to let go.

How to Quit

Okay, so you've seen the light and realised that numerical targets are bad for you and those around you. You want to give them up, but you've been using them for years. How do you overcome the cravings that you are likely to experience? Well, you might want to explore the options in this 'official advice' from the Stick People:

General Advice: Now, the first thing to appreciate is that giving up targets is not going to be easy, especially if you've had a serious targets habit for some time. Some managers have gotten to the point where they are on 40 targets a day.

This level of addiction can make it even more difficult to go without targets at first, but recognising you have taken the first step towards ridding yourself of these evil little blighters is a great start. It might feel like your comfort blanket has been cruelly pulled away from you, but in the long run you'll know that it was the right decision.

Don't be tempted to snatch the blanket back and give it a little cuddle. Relapsing for the sake of even one target 'just to be social' could easily drag you back to where you were – don't be tempted.

Patches: There are various products out there on the market to help you ditch your targets habit, once-and-for-all. For example, these 'target' patches are quite popular:

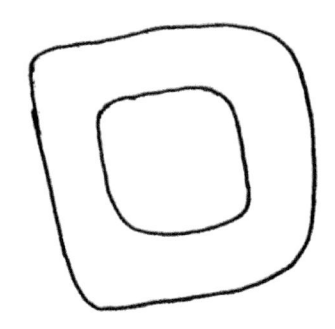

Each patch contains a small amount of the highly-addictive chemical *targetine*, which is found in all numerical targets.

Using the patches can soften the impact of suddenly giving up targets, as they release ever-diminishing doses of targetine as the user progresses through the course. Results, however, can vary.

Other Products: Another popular method involves the use of *substitute targets*. In a similar way that substitute cigarettes offer the user a realistic look and feel of a genuine cigarette, a pack of substitute targets allows the user to experience the thrill of looking at arbitrary numerical targets without any of the harmful side effects.

A typical pack of substitute targets looks like the example below, which happens to be a police example. There are now a wide range of these products available to suit many types of target addiction; these include substitute targets for hospital waiting times, exam results, and service level agreements for correspondence – in multiples of '7 working days', '15 working days', or '28 working days (excluding Bank Holidays)'.

	REDUCTION TARGET	ACTUAL	DIFFERENCE	TREND
TOTAL CRIME	-5%	-4.6%	0.4%	↑
ROBBERY	-6%	-3.5%	2.5%	↑
ASSAULT	-8%	-4.1%	3.9%	↑
CRIMINAL DAMAGE	-10%	-6.5%	3.5%	↑
VEHICLE CRIME	-6%	-6.1%	0.1%	↓

As you can see, this option offers those suffering from withdrawal symptoms the opportunity to stare at numerical targets and worry about how to get the figures up by the end of the month without actually suffering any adverse side-effects.

This is only possible because all these targets are completely made up out of thin air, just like real ones, so it is impossible to know the difference. Extra comfort can be drawn from pretending that any positive 'trends' are real and came about as a result of dynamic leadership.

Some manufacturers also offer products for managers who suffer from the deadly condition known as 'league tables withdrawal' or are trying to overcome an addiction to binary comparisons. In a survey, 87% of 15 participants said they *"could not tell the difference between these substitute products and the real thing"*. Now *that's* science!

Hypnotherapy: A fourth option is to undergo 'targets hypnotherapy'. Studies report mixed success rates, with some people being completely cured, to the extent that they immediately start using control charts to see what the data are actually telling them about performance, rather than just guessing what the figures mean, or demanding improvement without a method.

Others are only partially cured. Often, these poor souls still believe that some targets must be okay, or that certain targets can be appropriate 'if properly implemented', whatever *that* is supposed to mean. The Stick People advise careful consideration before undertaking this method.

Stop!

Actually, none of these methods are any good! The only way to effectively distance yourself from targets is to use WILLPOWER.

Good luck. You'll be glad you quit!

The Wrong Conversation

Stick Child has been getting increasingly irritated by the slack methods some adults use to present information about really important stuff, such as how long it takes for patients to be seen in Accident and Emergency (A&E) departments.

Many a time recently he's had to do a facepalm at the way hospitals and other institutions are judged and compared against each other, supposedly to inform the public about how well each is performing.

The problem is that the starting point of the conversation – the frame by which performance is judged – is totally wrong.

Plenty has been written about the arbitrary nature of numerical targets and their propensity for triggering dysfunctional behaviour, so we'll leave that to one side for now, and just look at why using them as the focal point for judging performance simply means people engage in the wrong conversation.

Stick Child has drawn a couple of charts, which plot the distribution curves of A&E admission times for two hospitals; Hospital 'A' and Hospital 'B'. You can see his handiwork on the next page:

HOSPITAL 'A': % EMERGENCY ADMISSIONS WITHIN 4 HOURS

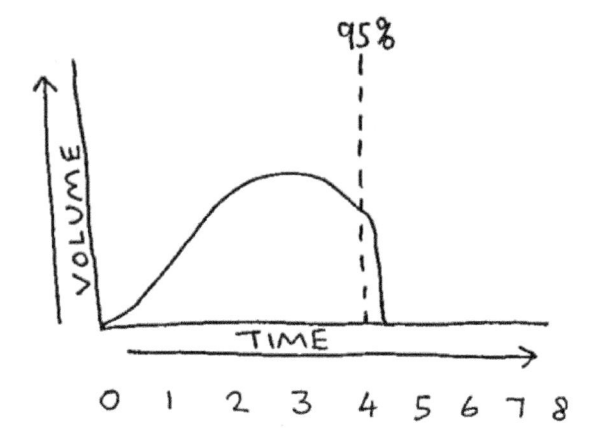

95%

Volume vs Time (0–8)

HOSPITAL 'B': % EMERGENCY ADMISSIONS WITHIN 4 HOURS

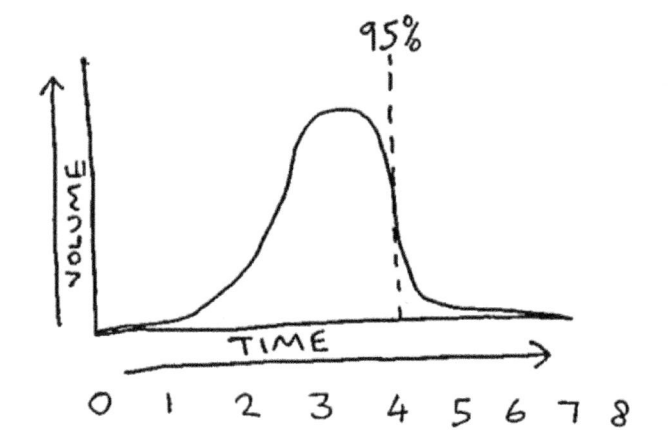

95%

Volume vs Time (0–8)

As you can see, the curves are different. Hospital 'A' manages to get 95% of patients seen within 4 hours, after which, a steep drop off in the curve indicates the remaining 5% are seen before 4 hours and 30 minutes has elapsed.

Hospital 'B' also manages to see 95% of patients within 4 hours, but the tail of the curve beyond this point is much longer, meaning that the remaining 5% of patients take much longer to be seen – some waits are as long as 7 hours. It's also apparent that Hospital 'A' sees more patients during the early stages of their wait than Hospital 'B'. This is evidenced by the fact that Hospital 'B's curve is weighted more to the right.

So, it's quite clear that the patterns of waiting times are different for the two hospitals.

Not according to the target.

According to the target, the two hospitals' performance is exactly the same. This means that opportunities to understand *why* some patients wait up to 7 hours in Hospital 'B' are missed. It means that managers don't get the chance to understand their system, as the usefulness of A&E admission time data is undermined by using the target as a focal point, thereby degrading potentially useful information into a simplistic PASS / FAIL scenario.

Now consider what would happen if Hospital 'A's distribution curve actually showed that 94.9% of patients were seen within 4 hours, whilst Hospital 'B' achieved 95.1%.

	% WITHIN 4 HOUR TARGET
HOSPITAL 'A'	94.9 %
HOSPITAL 'B'	95.1 %

Yes, despite the fact that Hospital 'A' demonstrates better overall performance, it FAILS, whilst Hospital 'B' PASSES. This fixation on the target and a binary definition of 'good' or 'bad' performance means no one learns anything about either hospital.

That's the real FAIL.

Then there's those convincing-looking charts which look authoritative, but actually spew out what can only be referred to as pseudo performance data, such as this:

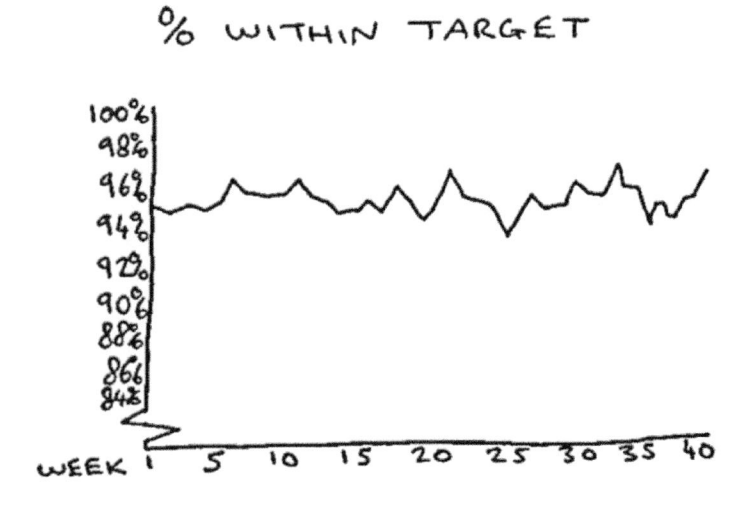

% WITHIN TARGET

Looks good, doesn't it? Well it's not. All it does is tell you the percentage of cases where performance has crossed that invisible and imaginary dividing line between 'good' and 'bad', as defined by the target. A chart that tells you about a target to hit a target. Utter waste of time.

If you've got the data, simply plot them and learn from them. Why throw in a target and thereby replace the richness of potentially useful performance information with a meaningless and mind-numbing YES / NO game? Seriously, why?

It drives the wrong conversation.

Stick Child and the Flat Tyre

Here's the problem – you have a flat tyre!

So, let's look at a couple of options for resolving this issue...

Method 1

One approach might be to inflate the tyre, then check the air pressure on a regular basis to see if it starts to go flat again. If it does, you could put more air in the tyre. Perhaps if the tyre still keeps going flat, you could increase the regularity of the air pressure checks and fill it with air more often. If, despite this, the tyre still keeps going flat, maybe you could shout at the driver a bit. That should do the trick! Problem solved.

Method 2

Another method might be to see what *caused* the tyre to go flat. In this case it was a nail, so you could just remove the nail, then either repair or replace the tyre.

Method 1 vs Method 2

I prefer Method 2, as it addresses the *root cause* of the tyre's flatness, rather than introducing disproportionate checks and unnecessary reactions which focus on the *symptoms*. Apparently, there are scientific studies that prove if you put a nail through a tyre, it is likely to go flat. Rocket science, this is not.

What the Pro-Nail Brigade Might Say

Now, Method 2 might seem logical to you and I, but there are people out there who disagree. For example, whilst you're trying to remove the nail, they might approach you and say things like:

"It's not the nail that's the problem because...

– It's the WAY the nail was inserted into the tyre.

– It must have been the wrong type of nail.

– It's the driver's fault for the way the car was driven whilst the nail was in the tyre.

– The nail needs to be there, otherwise air would leak out of the hole.

– Lots of nails would be bad, but there's only one nail in this tyre and that's okay.

– But I've always put nails in tyres / they look nice.

– I use things that might look a bit like nails, but they're called something else, so that's okay".

– It has to be something else, anything else. Nails don't cause flat tyres!"

The same people usually think the solution is to leave the nail where it is and blame individuals, introduce tougher sanctions, invoke more audit and inspection, or produce lots of meaningless numbers which they think will tell them about the air pressure. Unfortunately, this totally misses the point.

As long as destabilising system conditions are present, no amount of knee-jerk reactions, denials, holding people to account, or audits will prevent dysfunction, such as misreporting of air pressure, imaginative re-definitions of what a 'nail' can be classified as, or worsening damage to the tyre.

Method 2 is better because it addresses the *system conditions* that cause the issue. This means that we have an opportunity to remove them and resolve the problem. Therefore, if you keep encountering unwanted phenomena within your system, simply trace the root causes and eliminate them.

And yes, I'm talking about numerical targets, league tables and binary comparisons!

Detox

Whilst flicking through TV channels recently, I came across a consumer advice programme, where the reporter was researching the effectiveness of self-administered 'detox' products. The TV crew followed her for three days as she consumed nothing but 'specially formulated' fruit and vegetable juice drinks of various colours. At the end of the experiment, she visited a nutrition expert to discuss the results.

I have recreated the conversation that followed, with the help of my Stick People...

The reporter seemed surprised...

The expert's assessment wasn't that well-received...

The exchange made me chuckle, as it reminded me of this sort of thing...

...which is usually followed by this:

Oh dear. As writer Aldous Huxley said in 1927:

> *"Facts do not cease to exist because they are ignored".*

Finding the Source

I've usually found that the people at the very top of organisations tend to be intelligent, articulate individuals who genuinely care about their organisation and want it to perform well. I've also discovered that those who advocate targets often do so in the honest belief that they are a necessary feature of performance management. It's ingrained in their thinking.

Something else that I've become increasingly aware of is a common theme amongst the comments made by these very senior people. Recognise any of these?

> **"I'm well aware of the problems that targets cause and don't disagree with your arguments".**
>
> **"Comparison against targets (or peers) is just 'management information' that gives me the starting point to ask questions".**
>
> **"At this level we don't pay that much attention to the actual targets".**
>
> **"But I'm convinced that targets improve performance – I've seen it".**
>
> **"It's not me. I *have to* set targets because *my* boss wants them".**

Let's have a look at these statements in more detail, to try and encourage a different way of thinking about the 'targets conundrum'.

"I'm well aware of the problems that targets cause and don't disagree with your arguments".

My response to this is usually, "Well get rid of them then!" It's simply about making a cost / benefit analysis to assess the risks involved. If you already know that targets are likely to cause gaming, cheating, data distortions and other dysfunctional behaviour, why retain them?

This normally leads onto a discussion about what else could possibly be out there if the targets are removed. The answer? MEASURES. Getting *measures* confused with *targets* is such a common – and fatal – mistake: they are TOTALLY DIFFERENT THINGS!

Next...

"Comparison against targets (or peers) is just 'management information' that gives me the starting point to ask questions".

I've heard this one a lot. The problem is that making comparisons against targets or peers (usually presented in simplistic tabular and / or binary formats) causes managers to ask the *wrong* questions. "Why is your team's performance worse than the other team?" / "Why have you got more crime on your sector than at this time last year?" / "Why haven't you hit your sales target for this quarter?"

Starting out from a limited and often poorly-presented dataset, then comparing performance against a numerical target or the fluctuating variables that are inevitable amongst peer performance, increases the likelihood of incorrect assumptions and ill-informed decision making.

Oh, and don't fool yourself that if you remove the target but retain an ethos of comparing performance between peers (or against some random point in history), this would be somehow better.

The 'league table' approach leads to many of the same misguided assumptions and behavioural dysfunctions as targets – in essence it is akin to working towards an arbitrary MOVING target, rather than a static one. Avoid!

"At this level we don't pay that much attention to the actual targets".

You know what? I really believe this to an extent. I suspect most senior managers easily understand that there's more to life than red or green arrows and don't lose sleep if a couple of performance indicators are half a percent short of the target this month. I also believe that they take other relevant information and evidence into account when considering performance, and usually have an appreciation of the overall context.

The problem is that as you go down the levels of hierarchical organisations, the obsession with hard numerical targets intensifies. By the time you get to the front line, believe me, people DO pay A LOT of attention to the actual targets. The targets then become a focus for activity, driving behaviour and creating a culture of unhealthy competition and individual blame.

"But I'm convinced that targets improve performance – I've seen it".

This can actually be true (sort of). Research (in particular that of Edwin Locke and Gary Latham) has shown that targets can sometimes 'improve' performance. The downside, however, is that this apparently improved performance cannot be sustained in the long term; also, such improvements tend to limited to simple, repetitive tasks, rather than meaningful performance outcomes within complex operating environments, such as in the public sector.

Furthermore, a range of evidence provides multiple instances of dysfunctional behaviour that occurs behind the scenes in order to attain this 'improved' performance.

Examples include 'teaching to the test', reclassifying crime figures, making arrests for 'easy' offences', holding back funds until the next quarter, 'hiding' hospital patients in ambulances, excluding exam entrants deemed unlikely to succeed, prioritising what is easy ahead of what is important, falsification of documents, as well as various other forms of gaming and cheating.

As a result of this, costs go up, morale goes down, intrinsic motivation is damaged, individuals and departments turn against each other, risk increases, interdependencies break down, waste overwhelms the organisation, customers receive a worse service, and the system malfunctions. (All whilst hitting the targets!)

So it goes back to the cost / benefit thing again. No matter how good you or your people are, these horrid consequences *will* occur when you throw targets into the mix. Is that apparent short term 'improvement' really worth the overall long term damage to the system? You decide.

"It's not me. I *have to* set targets because *my* boss wants them".

This is perhaps the most interesting one to me. As a Police Constable I remember my Sergeant bemoaning targets, but saying that he couldn't do anything about them because they were 'what the Inspector wanted'. I hear Inspectors bemoaning targets but accede on the basis that they 'must have them because the Superintendent wants them'.

If you follow the trail to the top of many organisations, you will find that some Chief Officers / Chief Executives / Managing Directors will acknowledge targets cause harm, but feel they are still somehow expected to have them.

It's a bit like this:

?
IT'S NOT ME. IT MUST BE ONE OF YOU LOT DOWN THERE.
IT'S NOT ME. IT'S THE NEXT LEVEL.
IT'S NOT ME. IT'S THE NEXT LEVEL.
IT'S NOT ME. IT'S THE NEXT LEVEL
REDUCE BY 3%
4.6 PER DAY
NO MORE THAN 6.4
WHY AM I SUBJECTED TO THESE TARGETS?
AIM FOR 17%
DO 5 PER WEEK
WITHIN 4 HOURS

In policing terms, it may be that the Police and Crime Commissioner insists on having targets. Does it stop there though? Some Police and Crime Commissioners will tell you that they don't agree with targets, but their Police and Crime Panel (the body that holds them to account) expect them to have some.

Or could it be those bodies charged with inspecting police forces performance? Or local politicians? Or the Government? Or the media? Or the public? Or is it just because 'that's what we've always done'?

So where do they really originate?

Well, if you believe targets must be an inevitable feature of performance systems, you might find that it is YOU who is inadvertently perpetuating them, not the person above you.

If so, do something about it!

Short Circuit

This is Stick Boss. Stick Boss is basically a good guy who cares about his organisation and wants the best for people. Unfortunately, he has a problem with his brain. This means that just as he's on the cusp of understanding how to make best use of his performance information, his brain short circuits and he reverts to the use of arbitrary numerical targets (and other associated abominations).

Let's have a look inside his head to see what goes on in there...

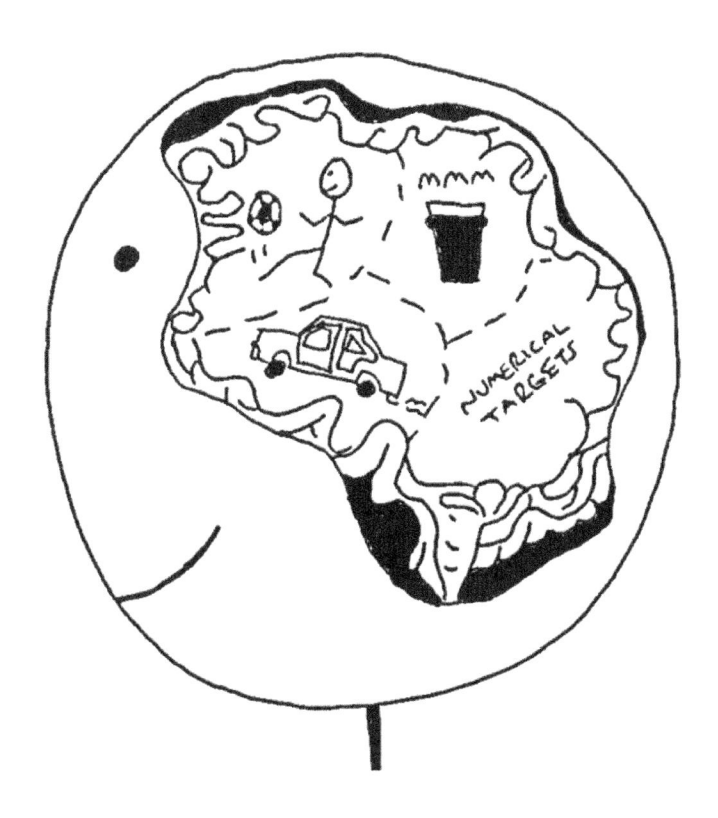

As you can see, the content of the different segments of his brain is pretty standard. Unfortunately, the 'numerical targets' quadrant interferes with his thought processes in certain circumstances.

Stick Boss is bright enough to understand that different parts of his organisational system influence each other, helping or hindering service delivery. Even some stuff that wouldn't be obvious at first can affect how well the front line performs. Therefore, Stick Boss is keen to understand where the opportunities for improvement lie, so he ensures his performance measurement system reaches into these dark backlots to extract useful information that can aid his decision making.

This is good. He's got a clear understanding of his organisation's purpose and recognises the need to have access to performance information that measures the right things.

But then the brain defect kicks in.

Instead of using the right measures in the right way, the short circuit in his brain overrides the need to present performance information in a usable, contextualised format, and supplants it with an ill-conceived reflex that results in his potentially useful data being corrupted by arbitrary numerical targets, league tables and binary comparisons. What a missed opportunity.

Like I said, Stick Boss isn't a bad guy, but his brain problem prevents him from realising the damage he is causing by relying on fundamentally illegitimate performance practices. So, if you know people like him, please help.

Stick Child's Kitchen Nightmares

One evening Stick Child was awake a bit later than usual and saw part of a programme about a TV chef who goes into failing restaurants and helps them get back on track. Being as Stick Child is only 9 years old, his Daddy quickly changed channels as the TV chef launched into a tirade consisting of language so colourful it would have made Stick Caligula blush.

Anyway, that night Stick Child had a dream that went a bit like this....

Stick Chef began to take a look around...

He didn't like what he saw.

And it got worse...

A violent rage began to erupt from within his stick body…

Stick Chef's meltdown continued…

Then he had a moment of calmness and clarity...

The other guy thought this sounded vaguely familiar, but listened anyway. Then things got even better...

The dysfunctional practices were no more and Stick Chef's work was done.

Then Stick Child woke up and smiled.

Why 'Year-To-Date' is Rubbish

'Year-to-date' figures are often used in performance frameworks, both in the public and private sectors. In policing, 'year-to-date' figures are regularly used to track the number of reported crimes at any given point in the year, supposedly as an indicator of whether the police are doing a good job or not.

Now, leaving aside the debate about whether crime rates should be used as a performance indicator at all, let's have a look at why the practice of 'year-to-date' itself is rubbish.

Imagine a runner...

Here we are – it's Stick Child's uncle, Stick Runner. Let's say he likes to run 12 miles at a time, and his personal best is 120 minutes and 1 second; an average of about 10 minutes per mile.

Next time Stick Runner sets out on a run, he aims to do his very best and see how quickly he can run the 12 miles. He knows that multiple factors will affect his performance, such as his fitness levels, his current weight, his choice of clothing, his diet, and so on.

He also knows that other, external factors will affect his performance; for example, the outside temperature, the wind, the terrain and so on. He might be held up for a few seconds waiting to cross a road. His shoelace might come undone. Something else might happen outside of his direct control that affects his final time.

So, Stick Runner sets out to maximise his chances of a fast time by ensuring the systems conditions he can influence are favourable. He trains. He doesn't run in a bulky duffle coat. He avoids drinking 10 pints of Guinness and eating a massive curry the night before his run.

Anyway, once he sets off on his run, Stick Runner is smart enough to measure progress, because he knows measuring stuff is vital. He wears a heart rate monitor which helps him check if his heart rate is within a normal and safe range. He checks his stopwatch every so often to gauge progress.

He processes this information as he runs along, taking into account the context around him, knowing that if his heart rate gets too high, he might have to slow down a little; likewise, he knows that when he's running along an uphill section of the route, he is likely to cover ground a bit slower.

Stick Runner uses all this information to ensure he is doing his best at all times. He knows that some miles will be faster than others, but is not unduly concerned because he understands this is normal. It might be that he beats his personal best this time, or it might be that he's just a few seconds too slow. Either way, his objective is to continually improve.

Now, imagine he adopted the 'year-to-date' method to pace himself – a strict 10 minutes per mile. Of course, this ignores all the factors that can influence his speed at any given time. So what happens?

Well, he completes the first mile in 9 minutes 55 seconds, giving him 5 seconds 'in the bank'. Unfortunately, the second mile is partly uphill and it takes him 10 minutes and 20 seconds, causing an overall 'deficit' of 15 seconds to that point.

Now the pressure is on, so he speeds up a bit, but realising he's still a bit behind time, he decides to sprint the last couple of hundred yards of the next mile. This makes him feel tired, but at least he makes up some time. This process repeats itself as he focuses on each individual mile, until he collapses at the side of the road, exhausted. Poor Stick Runner.

Clearly, no self-respecting runner would prefer that method over Stick Runner's original approach. But wait! Bizarrely, the equivalent of worrying about individual mile timings (and sudden sprinting) is prevalent in many performance management situations, as we shall now see...

The problems with 'year-to-date' are many, especially when today's figure is compared to:

- The average.
- The previous year's figure (or an aggregation of previous years' figures).
- An arbitrary numerical target.

Have a look at the table below:

	J	F	M	A	M	J	J	A	S	O	N	D	Total
This year	38	45	44	36	37	41	44	37	39	44	36	39	480
Monthly avg	40	40	40	40	40	40	40	40	40	40	40	40	480
Variance (vs monthly avg)	-2	5	4	-4	-3	1	4	-3	-1	4	-4	-1	0
Last year	35	43	42	40	38	39	45	38	40	37	38	45	480
Variance (vs last year)	3	2	2	-4	-1	2	-1	-1	-1	7	-2	-6	0
Target (reduce by 10%)	36	36	36	36	36	36	36	36	36	36	36	36	432
Variance (vs target)	2	9	8	0	1	5	8	1	3	8	0	3	48

Here we can see two performance years that ended neck-and-neck. (It doesn't matter what the numbers relate to). Firstly, imagine the reaction each month as management compare the 'year-to-date' figure with the monthly average required to finish the year 'on track' – Cue a mix of concern/anger/confusion (when it's higher), and feelings of success and self-congratulation (when it's lower). All of this, as you can see, is a big waste of time because looking at the whole year in retrospect, both rows come in at 480 anyway.

This occurs because of normal variation – the fluctuations amongst the numbers are caused by all those internal and external factors that affect how the system performs, as in the case of the stick person. As you can see, variation even applies to systems or processes that are stable. Therefore, there is no point whatsoever in getting excited about whether a number is a bit higher or lower than the average at any given point in time.

> *"About half of everything is below average",* as I like to say...

The misguided belief that some meaning can be ascribed to the types of fluctuations I've just talked about leads to exhortations such as, "We cannot afford to record more than 135 crimes per day", or "Sales must exceed £150,000 per week", and so on. It causes people to withhold surplus units of whatever's being measured until the next period. It causes under-recording and other bizarre practices designed to keep the numbers under control. This is equivalent to stick person disregarding his knowledge about his surroundings and running flat out.

And that's just comparing the 'year-to-date' figure against averages...that's bad enough, but check this out – what happens when you compare it against last year's 'year-to-date' figures? I'll tell you – it gets worse!

This is because – guess what – last year's figures were subject to variation too! The numbers went up and down. Crime, sales figures, unemployment rates, you name it – none of them happened in a nice flat line. We have ZIG ZAGS, people; ZIG ZAGS!

However, do not be alarmed – this is just normal variation again. So, when we try and compare this year's 'year-to-date' figure against last year's this is even dafter than making a comparison with the average because we are comparing two moving variables. Cue wider fluctuations and more panic...

Finally, we consider the comparison between the 'year-to-date' figure and an arbitrary numerical target – in this case a nice 10% reduction. As you can see from the table, the target was only achieved during two months.

This is because someone invented it in their head, without having any understanding of the systems conditions likely to influence performance. It's just like our runner suddenly setting himself a target to run 9-minute miles, when he has never run faster than 10-minute miles.

Targets do not provide a method for achieving stated aims.

Summary

All of these 'year-to-date' methods are incapable of telling you anything about performance. FACT.

Furthermore, they are all quite capable of inducing dysfunctional behaviour, as people mistakenly assume there must be a meaning for the apparent differences between the numbers (caused by normal variation), then change tactics to try and get the 'year-to-date' figure on the preferred side of whatever number it is being compared against.

'Year-to-date' obscures genuine trends when they do exist, causes false signals and mistaken assumptions, makes people ask the wrong questions about the wrong things, causes unfair blame and arbitrary praise, leads to short-termism, knee-jerking and a fixation on today's isolated number at the expense of understanding what the actual influencing factors are.

Oh, and you may have noticed – the whole approach is based on making *binary comparisons*, which are known to be very rubbish indeed.

So, if you use 'year-to-date' in your performance framework, do yourself a favour and ditch it immediately, then go out and do something useful with your data instead.

The Professionals

File photo: Armed Stick Police

Imagine a police force that handed out firearms to its officers without training them.

Or one that chose to opt out of established good practice for investigating serious crime.

Or one that refused to work with partner agencies because it didn't feel like it.

Or a force that allowed untrained officers to pursue criminals at high speed in fast cars.

The consequences would be predictable and these sorts of irresponsible actions would quite rightly attract criticism and incredulity.

So why is it any different for performance management?

How can individuals be expected to use performance information wisely when they don't fully understand it because they've never been trained? How can some managers be allowed to ignore the widespread evidence that dysfunction is likely to result from certain practices, such as the use of numerical targets, binary comparisons or league tables? Why are untrained people handed such responsibility and just expected to ask the right questions about the right things?

It's time to professionalise police performance management.

Leaders at all levels must be equipped to ask different questions, using legitimate forms of performance information as a starting point for understanding the whole system – they also need to stop asking for products that are fundamentally illegitimate, simply because they are comfortable with the format.

Decision makers require trusted expert analysts to act as specialist tactical advisors, providing them with fit-for-purpose, contextualised performance information. It's no different to calling in expertise from hostage negotiators, search specialists, firearms or public order tac advisors.

The police service needs clear national guidance and bespoke training programmes that provide leaders with a real understanding of performance measurement and management, along with its implications.

We need to completely reframe and reorient the performance conversation from one that fixates on simplistic concerns about whether something appears to be 'good' or 'bad', to one that uses performance information as an evidence base for making good decisions, understanding, learning and improving. We need to stop trying to out-do each other, blaming individuals and using the wrong mechanisms to ask the wrong questions about the wrong things.

Managing complex investigations, running firearms operations and driving fast cars requires high levels of training, professionalism, and responsibility.

It shouldn't be any different for performance management.

A Better Way

One day during the school holidays, Stick Child's Daddy took him to an outdoor adventure park, where people climb through the trees using various ropes, nets, rickety bridges, zip wires and other things. Stick Child's Daddy thought he'd be pretty good at it, as he'd been on similar obstacle courses when he was much younger...

It soon became apparent, however, that he was a lot slower than his boy, moving with all the grace and finesse of a large land mammal, tangling himself up in his safety ropes and wobbling precariously as he crossed from one platform to the next. Also, the higher they went, the wobblier he became, hugging the tree trunks desperately and avoiding eye contact with the ground.

Stick Child thought this was quite funny and was tempted to laugh at his Daddy, who had been acting all big and tough when they were on the ground. Instead, he decided to help him, as he had learnt some good techniques for tackling these sorts of obstacles on a recent school trip.

At first, Stick Child's Daddy still thought he knew best ("I've been doing it this way for years, Son"), but Stick Child showed him some simple techniques that enabled him to traverse the obstacles a lot more quickly and surefootedly. Some of the techniques were a bit counter-intuitive to Stick Child's Daddy and he was quite nervous at times, as his natural reaction was to grab onto obstacles when Stick Child told him that going across 'hands free' would give him better balance and speed.

It was scary at first, but Stick Child's Daddy trusted his boy, and found the alternative approaches worked much better. Father and Son had a great afternoon and the elder of the two learnt a lot as well.

So, this happy tale is likely to have a badly-hidden moral or two, isn't it?

Here you are then...

1. If you've been using targets, league tables and binary comparisons to manage performance, then it's natural to want to keep doing what you've always done (or what others do) – it's also natural to be nervous about alternative approaches, because that means you're going to have to jump off the platform and fly down that zip wire. Just do it!

2. If you're one of those people who already knows about Stick Child's techniques, then it's better to share the knowledge with those ungainly (but probably well-intentioned) folk who struggle to move deftly through the trees, rather than just point and laugh at them. They might react with denial, annoyance, embarrassment or even jealousy at first, but hopefully they'll eventually see for themselves that there's a better way of achieving the things they've always been trying to achieve.

About the Author

Dr. Simon Guilfoyle is a serving police officer, who holds a PhD in police performance management; his research specifically focuses on the behavioural implications of the use of different forms of performance information.

He has authored a number of published articles on this subject, as well as a 2013 book, *Intelligent Policing*. He designs and delivers lectures and training on his specialist subject and works to promote Systems Thinking approaches in UK policing and beyond.

In his spare time he carries heavy backpacks across arduous terrain in horrible weather, for fun. He also likes to drink beer, listen to music and make curries, often simultaneously.

Printed in Great Britain
by Amazon